VINTAGE ELEVENS

A. A. Thomson

VINTAGE ELEVENS

PELHAM BOOKS

First published in Great Britain by
PELHAM BOOKS LTD.
26 Bloomsbury Street
London W.C.1
1969

7207 0203 8

Set and printed in Great Britain by Tonbridge Printers Ltd, Peach Hall Works, Tonbridge, Kent, in Garamond eleven on thirteen point, and bound by James Burn at Esher, Surrey

Acknowledgements

Thanks are due to the following for permission to reproduce the photographs indicated: *Radio Times Hulton Picture Library* 1, 4; *The Mansell Collection* 2, 28; *Press Association* 3, 9, 18, 30, 32, 40, 43; *Sport & General* 5, 6, 7, 13, 15, 20, 22, 23, 29, 31, 44, 46; *Central Press* 8, 10, 11, 12, 14, 16, 17, 19, 21, 24, 25, 26, 27, 33, 34, 35, 36, 37, 38, 39, 41, 42, 45.

Contents

FOREWORD 11

1 Derbyshire, 1936 13

2 Essex, 1897 18

3 Glamorgan, 1948 24

4 Hampshire, 1961 30

5 Gloucestershire, 1876 36

6 Kent, 1910 41

7 Lancashire, 1928 47

8 Leicestershire, 1967 53

9 Middlesex, 1947 60

10 Northamptonshire, 1912 68

11 Nottinghamshire, 1929 75

12 Somerset, 1966 82

13 Surrey, 1955 89

14 Sussex, 1932 95

15 Warwickshire, 1911 *by Denzil Batchelor* 102

16 Worcestershire, 1964 *by Denzil Batchelor* 109

17 Yorkshire *by Denzil Batchelor* 117

Index 124

Illustrations

1	C. J. Kortright	*facing page* 20
2	P. A. Perrin	20
3	Frank Woolley	20
4	Colin Blythe	20
5	W. G. Grace	21
6	Roy Marshall	28
7	Derek Shackleton	28
8	Hampshire, 1961	28
9	George Duckworth	29
10	Charlie Hallows	29
11	E. A. McDonald	29
12	M. R. Hallam	32
13	Leicestershire, 1967	32
14	Bill Edrich and Denis Compton, 1947	33
15	Middlesex, 1947	33
16	George Gunn	48
17	Harold Larwood	48
18	Bill Voce	48
19	Somerset, 1966	49
20	Bill Alley	49

21	Fred Rumsey	49
22	Alec Bedser	64
23	Peter May	64
24	Surrey, 1955	64
25	James Langridge	65
26	Maurice Tate	65
27	K. S. Duleepsinjhi	65
28	W. G. Quaife	80
29	Worcestershire, 1964	81
30	Tom Graveney	81
31	Len Coldwell	81
32	Herbert Sutcliffe	96
33	Bill Bowes	96
34	Kent v Yorkshire at Tonbridge	96
35	Hedley Verity	97
36	W. A. Copson	97
37	J. C. Clay	97
38	Jim Sims	97
39	Brian Sellers	112
40	A. W. Carr	112
41	Stuart Surridge	112
42	A. W. Richardson	112
43	Wilf Wooller	113
44	R. W. V. Robins	113
45	Don Kenyon	113
46	A. C. Ingleby-Mackenzie	113

Foreword

He was my friend.

When A.A. Thomson died in June, 1968, he had completed all but three of the chapters for this book. The three counties still to be covered were Warwickshire, Worcestershire and his beloved Yorkshire. Denzil Batchelor, a very old friend of 'Tommie's', thereupon agreed to complete the series. I am most grateful to him and to the Editor of *Playfair Cricket Monthly* for allowing Pelham to reproduce the last three chapters in this book – an action which 'A. A.' himself would certainly have appreciated.

Only two years ago 'A. A.' recorded in an interview in W. H. Smith's *Trade News* how it was he came to take up his pen in order to set down for the lasting pleasure of hosts of cricket fans his boundless enthusiasm for The Game.

'I was playing in a match at the Swanwick Writers' School,' he said. 'Bill Luscombe and I were fielding and swapping cricket yarns. Suddenly Bill said "Why don't you write these down?" "I have" I told him "but nobody wants them." "I want them" said Bill – and I've been tied to his tail like a kettle ever since.'

What happy years they were.

'Tommie' was a humorous writer for 40 years. For over 20 years he wrote 'Strolling Commentaries' for *Radio Times,* and contributed for two decades to *The Passing Show* as well as writing for *The Humorist, London Opinion* and *Punch.*

Of the 60 books he wrote his favourite without doubt was *The Exquisite Burden,* an account of his Yorkshire boyhood. Indeed, as I write that I can almost hear him saying with a quiet chuckle: 'Good, I'm *glad* you recorded that!'

He loved and relished the characters who took part in cricket, and his books on the subject were full of anecdotes which illuminated or enriched his story. His enthusiasm was tireless, his ability zestfully to portray character made his books a never failing source of delight. They earned for him an MBE in 1966. 'But' he said, unable to resist a joke, 'most of my friends can't read; and those who can, read *The Guardian. They* spelt my name wrongly, so nobody knew it was me!'

He was, however, deeply proud of the honour – just as he was of the letter he received from P. G. Wodehouse when *Cricket: The Wars of the Roses* was published. 'What a wonderful jacket they have given you' wrote Wodehouse. 'Not to compare with the contents, though. By the way, would Pelham Books like to use that as a comment? If so, tell them to go ahead.'

I record it here in order that readers may appreciate the range of admirers of 'Tommie's' writing. Just as long as there is cricket – and longer – he will be remembered with affection and gratitude.

He was my friend, and life holds nothing better than true friendship.

William Luscombe
Editorial Director
Pelham Books Ltd

Chapter One

DERBYSHIRE, 1936

I might perhaps have started with my own county, but, if you remind me that charity begins at home, I could reply that Yorkshire, with 29 championships in their cricket-bags, are less in need of charity than anybody else on earth. Rather would I glance at a near and sturdy neighbour, Derbyshire, where the mountain scenery is enchanting, industry is robustly lively and the folk, on their own confession, are strong in the arm and, let us say, hard in the head.

The year of Derbyshire's vintage eleven is 1936 and the players are: A. E. Alderman, D. Smith, T. S. Worthington, L. F. Townsend, H. Storer, C. S. Elliott, H. Elliott, A. W. Richardson, A. V. Pope, T. B. Mitchell and W. H. Copson. No county wins high honours without an eager reserve or two, but these names form the steel framework.

There is an interesting theory that the cricket of any age mirrors that age's historic and social background. This, for the middle 1930s at least, I beg leave to doubt. The 'thirties, which gave us so much delightful cricket, covered a period of menace abroad and heavy unemployment at home. Indeed, but for the hard times in the mines and mills of South Yorkshire, Nottingham and Derbyshire, there are many illustrious players who might have remained no more than jolly club cricketers.

In an age that was socially drab Derbyshire cricket shone with a hard, clear flame. They were, in cricket terms, a 'small county, with a small administration, a small staff and limited financial backing, yet in that year of 1936, with Middlesex and Yorkshire breathing down their neck, they battled their way to the head of the table. This was the first time they had reached the top, unless you count what their present secretary has called 'the rather dubious victory' of 1874, a victory which *Wisden,* perhaps yielding to ghostly prodding from the shades of W. G. and E. M. Grace, now officially attributes to Gloucestershire.

About 1936 there is no argument. Derbyshire won on merit, if any side ever did. In the first place they possessed two major ingredients, without which you will not have a vintage eleven. The celebrated C. B. Fry was once asked (I think foolishly):

'Is it true, Mr Fry, that you were a great captain?'

'Of course I was a great captain,' said Fry. 'I had great bowlers.'

The reply was three parts humorous and only one part arrogant, but it enshrined a vital truth. Supreme success depends first on bowlers of commanding quality and then on commanding leadership. Obvious examples of this truth leap to the eye in the Surrey of Surridge and the Yorkshire of Sellers, where the bowling was varied and powerful and the captaincy was forceful in a way that had seldom been seen before and has scarcely appeared since, though Brian Close frequently reflects flashes of it. Among counties not so blessed as Surrey and Yorkshire, or at any rate not blessed so often, the Derbyshire of 1936 were not lacking in the two basic components.

These were: the wonderfully varied bowling of Copson, Mitchell, Townsend and A. V. Pope, added to the vigorous leadership of A. W. Richardson, who drove his coach and mettlesome horses with a light rein in a firm hand. Of their triumph there is no doubt, but it contained some ironical undertones. For instance, George Pope, in later years the county's most notable all-rounder, damaged a cartilage and did not play after May, while Denis Smith, their most dashing batsman and on the previous season's accomplishments having been chosen as a Cricketer of the Year, suffered a long, unluckily sticky patch and seemed to mislay his knack of hitting hundreds until August. They had some handsome all-rounders like Worthington and Townsend, but in their handsomest year, nobody did the double.

Moreover, none of the records of which any county is normally so proud occurred in this year: highest totals, best partnerships, biggest individual scores, most wickets in a season, any achievement you like to name. Denis Smith, for instance, had a double century in 1935 and another in 1937, but not one in 1936. Worthington, their most successful batsmen, with 1734 runs, came only fifteenth in the first class averages. You could even say, if you were prepared to duck and run quickly, that they performed one important feat: they won the championship and they won it because, above all things, they were a team.

This was the sixth season that they had played under Richardson and their more recent progress had displayed all the drama of a rocket-site countdown: in 1934 they came third; in 1935 second and in 1936 first. There was an inevitability about it.

They were, as I say, a team, and there was no system, but this does not mean that they had no outstanding players. Worthington, who had earned four caps against New Zealand as early as 1929, was twice capped against India in Derbyshire's championship year and on the strength of an average of 107 was picked to visit Australia with G. O. Allen's unlucky side the following autumn. Here he played creditably in three Tests, going in first with Barnett. Denis Smith had worn two England caps against South Africa the year before, and Copson, H. Elliott and Mitchell were all at various times capped players. Why an England place was never found for so fine an all-rounder as Townsend who did the double three times (though he did not manage it in 1936) has always puzzled me.

Their success comes back to teamwork, captaincy, and hostile bowling. Though their batsmen did not monopolise the first class averages, their bowling was a different cup of tea. In the bowling figures Copson, who took 160 wickets, came third, only yielding pride of place to the supreme masters of the period, Larwood and Verity. Alf Pope, with 99, and Mitchell, with 121, were not all that far behind him, while Townsend, who captured 63 wickets as well as making 1514 runs, was a shining example of how to display both skills.

Copson was a link in Derbyshire's strong chain of fast or fast-medium bowlers which stretches from Warren and Bestwick before him to Gladwin and Jackson and Harold Rhodes; it has been a chain curiously comparable with Yorkshire's chain of slow left-handers, from Peate, Peel and Rhodes to Roy Kilner and Verity. Copson, whose fiery red hair matched his fiery bowling, can still be seen standing as a first class umpire and his hair has not by any means become completely grey. He was one of those who left his coal-mining job during the general strike of 1926 and worked his way up through his colliery club into the county eleven. Success does not often come to a bowler with the first ball of his first match but that is what happened in 1932 in Derbyshire's match with Surrey at the Oval. Sandham was his first victim and further scalps were taken from Shepherd, Jardine and Fender. From then on he never looked back and was playing for England as late as 1947. He bowled faster than medium pace and could make the ball whip up or back alarmingly. You would not think to look at him now that in his early playing days his health was not good and it is pleasant to recall that the county helped to see him through this awkward period, so that by the time he retired he had taken well over 1,000 wickets.

The success of A. V. Pope was a kind of compensation for the long absence of his more exuberant brother George, and he bowled like a Trojan, sending down nearly 1,000 overs, and it is obvious that a man who took exactly 99 wickets in a season must have suffered a good bit of bad luck, and borne it cheerfully.

But the really deadly combination came with Copson's brimstone at one end and Tommy Mitchell's treacle at the other. There was a seductive element about his slow, cunningly flighted leg-breaks which tempted the most cautious batsmen into near-madness. In his career he must have made 1417 of these chaps look foolish and, as a 'character', he was just about the loamiest, most rumbustious between Emmott Robinson and Freddy Trueman.

One more point puzzles me. These heroes of 1936 were hardly any of them in the first flush of youth. The 'baby' of the side, the only one under 27, was C. S. Elliott, now a highly respected member of the umpires' Test panel, who was 24; their immensely gifted wicket-keeper, Harry Elliott, who played for England four times, was 41, and the average age, if I have worked it out correctly, was 31. Parenthetically, they must have been a respectable lot, because four of them, Alderman, Copson, C. S. Elliott and, if you will allow me a twelfth man, George Pope, are first class umpires today.

There they were, winning thirteen matches and drawing eleven, often owing to bad weather. Of the four games they lost two were to Somerset, who have never won a championship, but specialise in tumbling champions.

Finally, the whole lot of them, who averaged 31 years 33 years ago, are all happily fit and well today.

Chapter Two

ESSEX, 1897

Essex, who have never won the championship, had their most successful summer in Queen Victoria's Diamond Jubilee year. This was only their fourth season since achieving first class status and to come third to the Lancashire and Surrey of that era was a genuine feat, though Essex played considerably fewer matches. The system of counting one point for a win, minus one for a loss and ignoring all unfinished games had a rough justice in it, as it finally bestowed the championship upon the county that obtained the highest number of points on finished games. You may argue that as Lancashire, Surrey and Yorkshire played 26 games and Essex only 16, Essex had a better chance of securing a better proportion. On the other hand, to play eight additional games may well have given more opportunities to stronger sides to pick up extra points cheaply from their lowlier brethren at the bottom of the table. The argument works both ways.

Essex since the second world war have never been higher than fifth. This happened in 1957, under the lively captaincy of D. J. Insole and the inspiration – I will use no lesser word – of Trevor Bailey, who headed the county's batting and bowling for the second time and did the double (his fourth) with 1322 runs and 104 wickets. The libellous legend that Bailey has bedevilled Essex will get no backing from me.

Their best inter-war season was the last, that of 1939, when their three leading batsmen were A. V. (Sonny) Avery, M. S. Nichols and Jack O'Connor, and their most successful bowlers the same Nichols plus the Smith kinsmen, Peter and

Ray. Nichols, who completed his eighth double with 1387 runs and 121 wickets, had had an even more prosperous season the year before, but had not helped his county to quite such success.

These two seasons, happy though they were, did not throw up so many rich personalities as the Jubilee year and the team that then took them to third position was richly endowed. 'Beyond all question,' said *Wisden,* for once grandiloquent, 'the most striking feature of the 1897 season was the rise of Essex . . .'

Grandiloquent or not, *Wisden* is strictly truthful. Essex were indeed a striking force. They beat Yorkshire twice and Lancashire the champions once, being very unlucky to lose the battle at Old Trafford. And all this with only a dozen cricketers normally available. This makes the choice of an eleven comparatively easy. It is only the position of twelfth man that presents difficulties. Of the sixteen games played, five played in all; seven in fifteen; eight in thirteen; nine in twelve; eleven in fourteen, and all in nine. The five who played in all matches were among the most illustrious ever to turn out for Essex; the batsmen, Perrin, McGahey and Carpenter, and the bowlers, Walter Mead and F. G. Bull, and C. J. Kortright, said, by those who saw him, to be the fastest in history.

The eleven would be: (1) F. L. Fane, (2) H. Carpenter, (3) P. A. Perrin, (4) C. P. McGahey, (5) A. J. Turner, (6) H. G. Owen, (7) T. M. Russell, (8) C. J. Kortright, (9) F. G. Bull, (10) W. Mead and (11) H. Pickett.

This leaves the old England player, A. P. Lucas, as twelfth man, but, already, he was over 40 and had been awarded the first of his England caps nineteen years before. Even though he appeared in ten of the 16 county matches and played two superlative not out innings of 59 and 57 against Surrey at the Oval, the fact remained that Perrin, McGahey, Turner and Fane were of a younger generation, not so much knocking as banging at the door.

I never saw this eleven in action – I would have been three years old at the time. When I first saw Essex play, H. G. Owen, the 1897 captain, had already retired, but his reputation came down without question as a fine batsman and a cheerfully able captain who did not need to be such a martinet as at least one later leader became. At all events Essex have never had quite such a strong batting side since then. Their openers were Fane, the young university blue, who was later to play in three Test rubbers, one in Australia and two in South Africa, and Herbert Carpenter, one of the famous Cambridgeshire Carpenters. This was a distinguished opening pair highly regarded in an era of distinguished opening pairs. Fane (Charterhouse and Oxford) provided the elegance and Carpenter the solidity. His batting had the same strength, though not quite the same distinction, as that of his father, who was one of the pioneers of the missionary Wandering Elevens.

There had always been Haywards and Carpenters in Cambridgeshire, one of the two or three most illustrious cricketing counties of the 1860s. As Cambridgeshire's pre-eminence declined, the Haywards turned up in Surrey, led by the famous Tom, and the name of Carpenter transferred itself to Essex. Herbert Carpenter, of our 1897 eleven, had the family correctitude and an enormous skill in back-play whether in cutting or forcing off his feet. Back-play, with less or greater degrees of skill, is a present-day convention; but at the turn of the century, when forward play of the classical kind still held sway, batsmen like Carpenter showed that both had their values. Such was his soundness that he was actually playing first class cricket in 1920 at the age of 51.

Compton and Edrich, those delightful spreaders of comfort and joy in post-war seasons, were not the inventors of twinship. Percival (more often called Peter) Perrin and Charlie McGahey were known as the Essex twins long before 1947. On our eleven their ages were 21 and 26, and, if ever Essex had a reputation for tediousness, it was not in their

Essex, 1897. *Left:* C. J. Kortright. *Right:* P. A. Perrin

Kent, 1912. *Left:* Frank Woolley. *Right:* Colin Blythe

Dr. W. G. Grace. When 'W.G.' captained Gloucestershire in 1876, he was
undoubtedly somewhat slimmer but just as commanding!

time. Their scores, separately or together, would fill a reasonably-sized record book. Perrin, over six-foot tall, had won his spurs the year before in his first county game against Surrey, scoring a brave half-century against the lightnings of Richardson and Lockwood. His height and reach made him a formidable driver and his gift for keeping his eye on the ball ensured a firm defence. Two tales are especially re-membered about him: that at Chesterfield in 1904 he scored 343 not out – his tremendous driving brought him 68 fours – *and yet finished on the losing side*. He is also remembered, with more than a little injustice, as a bad fielder. This ex-aggerated description brought him the reputation of being 'the best batsman who never played for England.' This is a phrase that irritates my normally placid surface; there were in those greater days many who never played for England, but who, if they were now at the height of their powers, would be dragged willy-nilly into the England eleven today. But the general argument leads nowhere in particular, and was, I think, best answered by the whimsical Alec Skelding who, when asked on a brains trust who was the best batsman who never played for England, replied emphatically: 'Don Bradman.' With equal emphasis I would say that Perrin was no slouch at a catch; in fact, he could and would hold everything in reach. His misfortune was his slowness of movement after the ball had passed him. Hence the apocryphal dialogue, following a long, slow chase to the Vauxhall end.

'Well, Peter, did you save the four?'

'Yes, I did. Mind you, they ran eight.'

McGahey, his 'twin' and partner in many a gay adventure, was also a six-footer with a punishing reach and the motto: 'Four off a bad ball and two off a good one.' He never appeared to be in a hurry, but often scored more quickly than those who looked to be lashing out all over the place. His habit of driving the ball straight back with terrific force once broke his partner's arm, which distressed him greatly, because he had the kindest of hearts. He made scores of well over

200 three times, but he reckoned that his best innings was the one played against Lancashire at Old Trafford the following summer when, set 336 to win in the last innings of a rather low-scoring match, he carried Essex to triumph by four wickets with a majestic innings of 145 not out, after he and Perrin hit 191 in partnership. This innings is reckoned historic even in the history of Old Trafford. In their 16 Essex matches of 1897 Perrin and McGahey scored, twin-like, 937 and 925. Their combined career totals amounted to over 50,000 runs and there was never, I will wager, a dull run among the lot.

Above these two masters in the county averages came A. J. Turner, then only 19, who, taking first class cricket in his stride, went from Bedford Modern School into the Army, ending up as a brigadier general with an outstanding war record. As little more than a schoolboy, he more than held his own with the veterans.

Of the wicket-keeper, Tom Marychurch Russell, it need only be said that for ten years he kept to the tremendous speed of Kortright and the infinite wiles of Bull and Mead. He also had time to become the father of one of the county's most prolific scorers, A. C. (Jack) Russell.

Essex generally operated with only three bowlers, but these three were the highest quality. C. J. Kortright was called, at least before scientific measurement became practicable, the fastest bowler who ever lived; at least, he was fast enough to have figured in most of the fast bowler stories, current between John Jackson and Freddie Trueman, though no other bowler has ever been credited, as was Kortright, with a six in leg-byes off the batsman's left ear. He was another of the fine cricketers who never played for England. (Question: 'Who was the fastest bowler who never played for England?' 'Learie Constantine.') The reason why some outstanding players fail to win Test caps is that one, or perhaps two, players of the same kind were even more outstanding. The reasons for Kortright's deprivation at his peak were two: Lockwood and Richardson. What happens to A in these instances is unfortunate for when B and C are ready to retire, the youngsters, D and E, are arriving, and Kortright, kept waiting by Lockwood and Richardson, was not young enough to compete with, say, Walter Brearley.

He kept his interests in cricket and golf intact into old age and his faculties at 80 were lively indeed. I heard him say at a time when the bowler was supposed to be labouring under insupportable difficulties: 'What's that? What's that? Haven't they got three stumps to bowl at?'

The other two bowlers, the amateur F. G. Bull and the tough professional Walter Mead, got through the majority of enemy defences. With Kortright they captured 236 wickets, all but 20 of those taken by Essex. Young Mr Bull was in that year, 'the bowler of the eleven'. He had all the gifts a mediocre slow bowler lacks: masterly length, natural spin, and a monkey's wealth of tricks. It was said of him that his spin was as much an inborn gift as an ear for music.

Walter Mead was a medium-pace bowler, in pace somewhere between the speed of Kortright and the slows of Bull; and possibly the most valuable of all. He could be fast medium or slow medium and you wouldn't know from his easy action until you had played too soon or too late. His energy was tireless and his humour was dry. He took 100 wickets in a season ten times and 17 in a match twice, one of them against an Australian touring side. When he died, his funeral was attended by crowds of cricket-lovers and the vicar, who preached the valedictory address, was eloquent if not strictly accurate. As he pictured Walter Mead in heaven, freed from all earthly sorrows, 'bowling away on a perfect wicket', a nearby mourner, one of the departed's bowling companions, uttered a compassionate groan.

'Perfect wicket?' he muttered. 'Why, that'll *kill* Walter!'

Since that day, the happening has been attributed to the obsequies of every bowler who, in life, liked a bit of help from the pitch.

But I think it suits Walter best.

GLAMORGAN, 1948

Glamorgan rose on merit to first class status in 1921 and, having got so far, wandered in the wilderness at least half as long as the Israelites of old. Between wars they languished in lowly regions and in that period were bottom of the table three times, second from the bottom five times and third from the bottom four times. Only twice did they find themselves in the top half of the table: in 1926, when they jumped from bottom to eighth place, and might have jumped much higher, and in 1937, when they rose to seventh. But all that time they never despaired; enjoyed, according to my information, endless fun, and from time to time displayed to the world such honoured names as N. V. H. Riches, now alive and hearty at 84; C. F. Walters, most graceful batsman of his time; Jack Mercer, invaluable all-rounder, and the ever-lamented Maurice Turnbull, who played nine times for England and gave his life in the second world war.

Though the loss of Turnbull left a cruel gap, they made brave efforts towards recovery immediately after the war. J. C. Clay, classical off-spin bowler, outstanding personality and indestructible survivor of the 1921 side took over the duties of honorary secretary and captain, captured 130 wickets and jollied his side up to sixth place. The following year was a Glamorgan landmark, for it saw the appointment to the captaincy of Wilfred Wooller, one of Wales's most illustrious Rugby footballers, an immensely gifted all-round cricketer, and a leader with wide strategic knowledge and something of the driving force of a Sellers or a Surridge.

In 1947 Glamorgan held the middle position and in 1948 they shot to the top. As almost always with triumphant teams, they were able to call regularly on the same eleven players, which gave them the advantage of combining together in match after match. It would be permissible to set down the eleven as: (1) E. Davies, (2) P. Clift, (3) W. G. A. Parkhouse, (4) W. E. Jones, (5) A. L. Watkins, (6) J. Eaglestone, (7) J. Pleass, (8) W. Wooller, captain, (9) L. B. Muncer, (10) H. G. Davies, (11) N. G. Hever. This, I say, would be permissible, but it would not be just, because it would mean leaving out the redoubtable J. C. Clay, whose baby rather than anyone else's Glamorgan cricket truly was; who had lived and worked in selfless enthusiasm for the day of victory, and who, though he appeared in only five games, played a vital part in the winning of the key match, against Hampshire in August, which clinched the championship. Therefore, though I try to choose my vintage elevens from those who played together throughout the season, I beg leave to nominate as twelfth man someone whose appearances have been fewer, but claimed recognition for special services. No man ever gave more special service than J. C. Clay.

Glamorgan's victory, though plainly well deserved, may well have caused a slight surprise among the prouder counties. Glamorgan did not glitter with individual names; indeed, their leading character is apocryphally credited with ironic reasons for victory: 'Bad batting and never winning the toss.' Ironic, yes, but containing a grain of fact: Glamorgan's batting was not full of Comptons and Edriches but it was good enough to give the bowlers time to get the enemy out, while to lose the toss fairly frequently gave the Welshmen the chance of knowing their target and chasing it ardently.

What the aphorism about bad batting and toss-losing omitted was the undeniable fact that Glamorgan's admirable bowling was backed by one of the most unforgiving phalanxes of close leg-side fielders that county cricket had ever seen. Such a ruthless grip was shown and exerted when, four years later,

Stuart Surridge started leading Surrey to the top. To teams visiting Cardiff Arms Park such a fielding machine was a revelation, and it was a machine which Wooller, the chief engineer, had constructed, set in motion, and kept in superb trim from the first game to the last. It was based on the theory of relentless on-side attack, operated by superbly specialist fieldsmen. Over 200 catches were taken and of these 135 were held by Watkins, Muncer, Clift and the skipper himself between them, close to the bat.

As we look at the 'bad' batting, we suspect that there was little wrong with a side that started with Emrys Davies and Philip Clift and then went on through young Gilbert Parkhouse, who scored a thousand runs in his first full season, and Willie Jones, more famous as a quick-footed Rugby footballer, but capable of heading his county's batting averages. Occasionally these batsmen forgot their intrinsic modesty and went to town in an outrageous way, as against Essex at Brentwood where they amassed 586 for five, including double-hundreds by Emrys Davies and Jones, who made 313 for the third wicket. Jones hit another hundred against Kent with the same ease as he displayed in dropping goals. He was left-handed as well as left-footed. Both these matches gave Glamorgan huge innings victories.

If you glance down the batting order you might wonder when it would start to become brittle: after Willie Jones, Alan Watkins, who that year played for England, the first Glamorgan player to do so, against Bradman's Australians. Unluckily, he got little out of this Test except a damaged shoulder, but his season's record of 1103 runs, 43 wickets and 40 catches, most of them at point blank range, showed the steely metal he was made of. During the season and for some years afterwards county colleagues and opponents reckoned Alan Watkins the most dynamic close fielder they had ever come across.

Next in order came Eaglestone, a batsman recruited from Middlesex, and Pleass, a local product, who both made useful scores at need, and, at No. 8, Wooller was in an ideal position to ride the whirlwind and direct the storm. Of the firm direction there was no shadow of doubt. Next came Haydn Davies, a wicket-keeper whose 16 stumpings displayed a guileful conspiracy with his slow bowlers, and bringing up the rear came the leading wicket-takers, Muncer and Hever, two more uninhibited immigrants from the metropolis.

The most remarkable thing about the bowling was not Muncer's 159 victims, but the fact that in county games six bowlers took more than 30 wickets apiece and in the full season's play they could say: 'We are seven'. Nobody could deny its variety. Muncer, bowling nearly 1,300 overs of his insidious off-breaks, was a master of spin and flight, and never paid much more than bargain prices for his wickets. There was no fast bowler in the sense that Miller and Lindwall, that summer making hay of England's batting, were fast, but Norman Hever and his captain would open the bowling with medium fast stuff and great spirit, while Jones (47 wickets), Watkins (43) and S. Trick (37) all took an effective turn with the ball. I had left Trick, a left-hand spinner from the South Wales League, out of my chosen eleven, because he played in only seven matches, but his name deserves to be set down, because he took 12 Somerset wickets in his first game and ten Kent wickets in his second. After that he unfortunately faded.

The person not to be omitted in any circumstances was without doubt J. C. Clay. After serving from Glamorgan's first first-class season until Glamorgan's first championship, he would have rejected the title of Grand Old Man, but though no man, especially a slow bowler, need call himself old at fifty, his service to cricket in South Wales and, indeed, to cricket as a whole, was without doubt grand. Throughout Glamorgan's sojourn in the lower reaches, cricket-lovers would always associate the name of Clay with Glamorgan's resilience. His was the head that, beneath the bludgeonings of fate, remained unbowed and not even particularly bloody. So in their year of triumph, though he played in only a limited number of matches, there was poetic justice in the fact that in the two vital August games he bowled with devastating effect, taking five for 15 and five for 51 against Surrey and nine for 79 in the innings victory over Hampshire that clinched the championship. The sporting Bournemouth crowd gave the Glamorgan players a rousing reception, but this was only an echo, though a pleasant one, of the ovation given them in their last home game at Cardiff, when they were acclaimed and applauded within an inch of their lives.

It would be impossible to exaggerate Wooller's contribution to victory. True leadership will always be a rare thing, and to be able to bat, bowl, field and direct involves more qualities than are generally to be found wrapped in one frame, however wily and vigorous. When runs were badly wanted, he would get them, as in the afore-mentioned 'Clay's match' against Surrey, when, after Glamorgan's first wicket had painstakingly collected 91, Wooller by tremendous driving hit 89 and only one other batsman scored more than six. In bowling he performed no spectacular feats, but you cannot send down nearly 900 overs and take 66 wickets in a season without having impressed your personality upon a number of batsmen and broken a number of resistances which made all the difference to the game. He called himself a stock utility bowler, but he was far more.

As for the fielding machine, he invented it and was an essential part of it. In the two matches which had the most critical bearing on the championship it was catching that finally settled the matter. In one match Clift held six catches and in another Watkins held five. At Trent Bridge against Notts Parkhouse held four in the first innings. Somebody, under his captain's gentle guidance, must have been wide awake somewhere.

Psychological warfare is not new. It was zestfully practised at the siege of Troy and in cricket it is at least as old as those amiable brethren, the Drs E. M. and W. G. Grace; but there

HAMPSHIRE, 1961. *Above left:* R. E. Marshall, one of County cricket's most attacking batsmen. *Above right:* Derek Shackleton, the mainstay of Hampshire's bowling for a decade. *Below:* The 1961 team: *Back row (l. to r.))* D. A. Livingstone, D. W. White, H. Horton, M. Heath, H. M. Barnard, M. D. Burden, P. J. Sainsbury. *Front row:* D. Shackleton, L. Harrison, A. C. D. Ingleby-Mackenzie (captain). R. E. Marshall, J. R. Gray

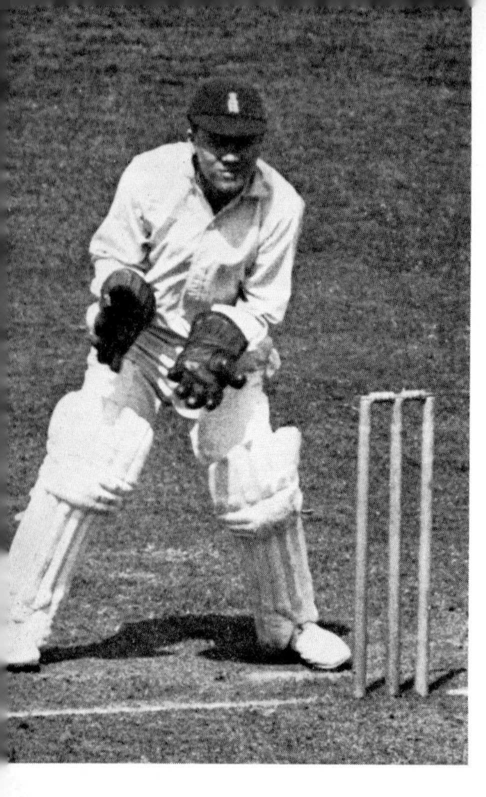

Lancashire, 1928. *Left:* The young George Duckworth, but already with an England cap. *Below left:* Charlie Hallows, who scored 1,000 runs in May 1928. *Below right:* E. A. McDonald, menace personified – to batsmen at least!

are many who still believe that Glamorgan's most astute post-war captain raised this form of more or less unarmed combat to perfection. 'In this facet of psychological warfare which is so much a part of first class cricket,' he has written, 'Glamorgan were not, I hope, ill-served.' And there are to this day some captains who, with rueful admiration, would regard this pronouncement as one of the leading understatements of cricket history.

It is hard not to return for a final word for the man who was in at the beginning and who actually bowled the ball that clinched the championship. When the delightful (and slightly incredible) happened, he rubbed his eyes and kept his fingers crossed, half-believing that there were fairies, if not at the bottom of the garden, at least at the end of the pitch. Such a man, in his skill, in his enthusiasm, in his untiring devotion, was indeed no common Clay.

Chapter Four

HAMPSHIRE, 1961

If Hampshire had not won the county championship in 1961 it might have been a delightful exercise to cheat a little and set down the Hambledon eleven of, say, two hundred years before. Hambledon, after all, was a Hampshire village and Hambledon – oh, my Nyren and my Beldham long ago – could be pitted against All England and beat them.

There was cricket in Hampshire all through the nineteenth century and when the county attained first class status in 1895 they had the fun of winning their first two matches and of beating Yorkshire by two wickets later in the season, a landmark in any county's history. Nineteen years later they came fifth, next to Yorkshire's fourth, but up the table or down, they always had fun.

Much of their enjoyment they owed to naval and military characters, now half legendary, like Captain E. G. Wynyard, who forced his way into a vintage England eleven in 1896, and Major R. M. Poore, who, the story went, would change into flannels as his troopship sailed up the Solent, march determinedly down the gangway, along the Northlands Road, and into the cricket ground to score 200 for Hants. (Years later, when told about the iniquities of body-line bowling, 'By gad,' he exclaimed, 'if they did that to me, I'd fix bayonets and charge the blighters!')

They obviously had the gaiety in their batting, but this was not matched in the bowling until the coming of C. B. Llewellyn, the all-rounder who might almost have had as many England caps as he fancied, if he had not been a South

African; later, between wars, they had one of the most effective of all county bowling pairs, Alec Kennedy and Jack Newman, (now a lively veteran of 80), under the adventurous banner of Lionel, Lord Tennyson.

The county had its struggles after the second war and Desmond Eagar, as captain and secretary, did Trojan work in getting cricket going again. When A. C. D. (Colin) Ingleby-Mackenzie took over the captaincy in 1958, leaving Eagar still in charge of the administration, Hampshire shot up like a rocket to second place, a position hitherto beyond their attainment. Up like a rocket, then down like the stick: in 1959, to eighth and in 1960, twelfth. Then, with again the authentic whoosh, up went the rocket again. Almost till the season's end there was a terrific running fight with – guess who! – Yorkshire and the characteristic oddity of their triumph was that, although Yorkshire beat them in their last match, the issue had already been decided in the previous game when Danny Livingstone took an excellent catch in the deep to get rid of Derbyshire's wicket-keeper, Bob Taylor, and the crowd surged over the turf at Dean Park to acclaim Hampshire's leap to the top for the first time in their 66 years of first class history. My information is that a certain amount of celebratory champagne was consumed and that when the winners came out to field on the same ground the following day their articulation as they said good morning was primly, even painfully, precise, and that their fielding being just as painfully precise, Yorkshire were 191 before the second wicket fell. Things like that, you know, must be, after a famous victory.

Who were these men of 1961, who had no glamorous soldiers, no unshakable world-batsmen, like Philip Mead, who scored over 55,000 runs and over 150 centuries, no Llewellyn, no classic pair, like Kennedy and Newman? They were: (1) R. E. Marshall, (2) J. R. Gray, (3) H. Horton, (4) D. A. Livingstone, (5) P. J. Sainsbury, (6) H. M. Barnard, (7) A. C. D. Ingleby-Mackenzie, captain; (8) L. Harrison, (9)

D. Shackleton, (10) D. W. White and (11) A. Wassell. Here I am frankly fudging a little, because in fact it needed fourteen to complete the vintage eleven, D. O. Baldry, from Middlesex, alternating with Barnard as a batsman, and either Heath or Burden, according to the state of the wicket, changing places with Wassell.

I have heard myopic critics call this a three-man team, wholly dependent on Marshall's batting, Shackleton's bowling and Ingleby-Mackenzie's luck. This is fiction. Marshall's brilliance is not to be disputed. For sheer entertainment I would still as soon watch him as any batsman in England. This was a batsman's year, in which seventeen of them scored 2,000 runs, but of the Hampshire heroes Marshall (2607) was only one; Horton (2329) and Gray (2034) were not far behind. Three batsmen made 2,000 and six, bringing in Sainsbury, Ingleby-Mackenzie and Livingstone, made 1,000. One batsman only? Absurd.

Derek Shackleton was, and remains one of the awesome phenomena of modern cricket, bowling his 1,500 overs a season as though he were playing them on the pianola. But, in spite of his 158 wickets, he did not (though at times nowadays it may appear so) bowl at both ends. He received wholehearted support from that wholehearted cricketer, D. W. (Butch) White, who puts every ounce of his considerable weight into every ball he bowls. He took 121 wickets and, though he did nothing as devastating as his nine for 44 against Leicestershire five years later, he never relaxed in his enthusiasm. He in his turn was supported by Burden, whose off-breaks brought him 50 wickets; by Wassell, who captured 66 with his left-hand slows, and Heath (63) who could bang them down hard, as required.

Right through the season Roy Marshall, who made five hundreds and the odd duck but never played a dull innings, was reliably partnered by Jimmy Gray, who was happy to play second fiddle. (So would I be with Menuhin.) When the pair put on 155 against Somerset, Gray's share was 38.

LEICESTERSHIRE, 1967. *Left:* M. R. Hallam, who scored most runs for the County in 1967 (1,355). *Below:* The 1967 team at Lords: *Back row (l. to r.):* D. Constant, J. Birkenshaw, R. W. Tolchard, J. Cotton, B. J. Booth, M. Norman, B. Dudleston, W. H. Ashdown (scorer). *Front row:* P. T. Marner, M. R. Hallam, G. A. R. Lock (captain), C. T. Spencer, C. C. Inman

The Middlesex twins, Bill Edrich and Denis Compton, going out to bat at the Oval in 1947, the glorious summer in which they broke almost every important batting record in sight. *Below*: MIDDLESEX, 1947. *Back row (l. to r.):* I. Bedford, A. Thompson, L. Gray, L. Compton, J. Robertson, S. M. Brown, J. Young. *Front row:* W. J. Edrich, F. G. Mann, R. W. V. Robins (captain), J. Sims, D. Compton

He was all summer the symbol of skilled and loyal support.

Henry Horton, the team's No. 3, has brought distinction to both summer and winter games. A Hereford man, he played for Worcestershire after the war and, moving to Hampshire in 1953, he has followed the business of thwarting Hampshire's enemies ever since. All that time he has given his county sterling service and, of course, if you play full back for Blackburn Rovers and then Southampton, you have to be a sterling type. He is not the most elegant of batsmen and at the wicket he takes up what the lawyers would call an *a posteriori* position, not unlike that of a diver half way through a jack-knife. But there are other qualities besides elegance which win matches. Henry Horton has the others.

The No. 4 was a native, not of one of the more famous cricketing islands like Barbados or Trinidad, but one of the Leeward Islands, and if on Antigua's best-kept cricket ground you had seen a solid, chunky left-hander and murmured: 'Mr Livingstone, I presume,' you would have been right. You would also have contacted an excellent West Indian cricketer, not as a rule sporting the customary Caribbean exuberance, but rather the sturdiness of an older cricketing breed and reminiscent, not of the brilliance of a Sobers or a Kanhai, but of something more native and natural to Hampshire, of the unforgiving, immovable Mead.

Peter Sainsbury, at No. 5, is another candidate for the long-service medal, who began as an all-rounder and is still going strong as a batsman who has not lost the knack of slow left-hand bowling, an accomplishment which occasionally fizzes up into a Gillette Cup man-of-the-match award. At No. 6 Michael Barnard sometimes played and sometimes Denis Baldry, but each did good service in turn and the pair put up 1,000 runs between them. No. 7 was the wicket-keeper, Leo Harrison, another of the old indestructibles who, when he resigned the gloves to young Brian Timms, came back at need, but served full time and overtime as captain of the second eleven, an organisation almost unique in its ability to spot young talent a mile off.

So we come back to three who do not make a three-man team, but who cannot avoid being key figures: Roy Marshall, who played for West Indies four times in 1951 and whom I watched at Lord's sixteen years later hitting 95 before lunch with every superb stroke in the book and some enchanting ones from the appendix; Shackleton, one of the unforgettable bowlers of history, and the captain whose combination of charm, daring and self-generated good fortune had never been seen since the golden youth of A. P. F. Chapman.

Shackleton is what is called a seam bowler. Seam bowling is the with-it, trendy thing in these days and, at its frequent mediocre level, one of the major boredoms of modern cricket. But the true question is not, and never was, whether you bowl fast, slow, medium, off-breaks or leg-breaks. It is simply whether you are a *good* bowler and Shackleton is a marvellously good bowler, even more marvellously good than Tom Cartwright of Warwickshire, whom I also rate highly. At forty-three he has played for twenty years, received two bene-fits, and taken well over 2,700 wickets, considerably more than any other post-war bowler, even Lock, Trueman and Statham. Indestructibility, that's the word. To the lay spectator, so smooth, so rythmically perfect is his action that every ball looks like the one before: to the bewildered batsman there is infinite variety of pace, flight, turn and lift that shows again and again who is master. I suspect he will outlive us all to be the ghostly bowler trundling away for ever before the soundless clapping host.

And in the young captain, as authentic a cavalier as his gallant predecessor, Lionel Tennyson, Hampshire had some-thing that hardly happens once in a generation. Here was a leader with a light heart and a by no means feather-weight brain, who had gaiety, dash and luck, all guided by a basic shrewdness. When he made cricket seem delightful fun, then was the sign for the enemy to look out. Hampshire were in fighting mood. His jokes, his predilection for the turf, his laughing philosophy were well known and appreciated at their English face value. ('Tell me, Mr Ingleby-Mackenzie, is it true that you insist on all your men being in bed by eleven?' 'Certainly. After all, play begins at eleven-thirty.') Above all, he had that air, impertinent but not arrogant, of wearing the cavalier's plume, that indefinable thing for which Roget cannot find a word and the French call *panache.*

Third-day declarations are tricky affairs and in recent years seem to have degenerated into something between the pointless and the downright silly. But Ingleby-Mackenzie's uncanny blend of judgment and luck was not unconnected with his service in the Royal Navy, where they set some store by such phrases as the 'Nelson Touch,' 'by Guess and by God' and 'the Dear little Cherub that sits up Aloft...' In 1961 an experimental law had disallowed the follow-on and a skilled assessment of the alternatives was needed. So nice did his perception become that more than half Hampshire's wins were the fruits of clever declarations. Ten sides were caught and only two got away. No donkey-driver ever dangled carrot with such dexterous deception. Against Somerset, after being led by over a hundred, he took advantage of a superb second-innings double hundred by Marshall to declare, setting the enemy a perfectly possible target, and getting them out in time. Against Notts he cut it even finer, Hampshire winning by 15 with three minutes to spare. Napoleon, who used to shoot his generals if they were unlucky, would have promoted Ingleby-Mackenzie to marshal's rank on the spot.

I saw Hampshire frequently six or seven years later. Marshall batted beautifully, Shackleton bowled eternally, but where was the plume, where was the *panache?*

Chapter Five

GLOUCESTERSHIRE, 1876

I cannot to this day imagine why Gloucestershire have never won the Championship since the days of the Graces. They came second with good teams in 1947 and 1959 and with a superb team in 1930. I invite you to contemplate an eleven that ran: (1) A. E. Dipper; (2) R. A. Sinfield; (3) W. R. Hammond; (4) C. C. Dacre; (5) B. H. Lyon, captain; (6) W. L. Neale; (7) C. J Barnett; (8) F J. Seabrook; (9) H. Smith; (10) C. W. L. Parker, and (11) T. W. Goddard.

This side surely had everything; it just happened that Lancashire, champions for the fourth time in the last five seasons, were, on figures, even better. You might argue that, strictly on results, Gloucestershire should have come first. On the original reckoning they would. The 1930 figures ran:

	P.	W.	L.	W. first inns	L. first inns	No res.	P.
Lancs.	28	10	0	8	5	5	155
Glous.	28	15	4	2	6	1	152

Under the old system, which gave one point for a win, minus one for a loss and nothing for anything else, Gloucestershire would have won the championship by 11 points to 10. On a percentage based on wins out of finished games, Gloucestershire would have only had 78.9, while Lancashire would still have stuck to their 100.

Gloucestershire were a superb side by any standard. Next

to Bradman, Hammond was the finest batsman in the world at the moment and entitled to a place among the half-dozen greatest cricketers in history; among the lesser mortals, Dipper, Smith, Parker and Goddard were already among England's best players; Sinfield and Barnett were to be capped later, and Dacre had been a gifted member of New Zealand's first touring side. Among the only four bowlers who have taken 4,000 wickets, Parker comes next to Rhodes and Freeman, while Tom Goddard only missed his 3,000 by 21. But their greatest asset, apart from Hammond's manifold gifts, was the combative spirit of their captain, Beverley Lyon, the nearest rival in resource, ingenuity and sheer magnetic force to Brian Sellers of Yorkshire, the liveliest leader of his period.

Lyon agreed with the celebrated Sammy Woods, that 'draws were no good to anybody, except for bathing'; when he was obliged temporarily to turn over the leadership to F. J. Seabrook, his orders were worthy of a Nelson: 'Five points for a draw are no use to us: we want eight every time!' If any county captain of today would issue commands of this kind, I would die happy. And, just by the way, this Gloucestershire tied their match with the almost invincible Australians in what was perhaps the most dramatic game ever played between a county and a touring side.

The other puzzle about Gloucestershire is that they never reached the top during the captaincy of G. L. Jessop, which lasted from 1900 to 1912. Like Grace and Hammond, he was among the tiny company of the very greatest and was for me, as a Yorkshire boy, one of the two or three outside our county to whom reverence was due. He was the mightiest of all hitters and a spirited leader, but the county never rose higher than seventh and that was in the first of his 13 summers. Even in 1906, when in the last match they beat Yorkshire by one run to give the championship to somebody else, they rose to no higher than ninth.

The fact remains, however, that Gloucester's true championship sides were the ones that headed the table in 1874, 1876 and 1877. On performance I prefer the middle one of these. Their record was astonishing: they did not lose a match, in that season or the next. They were all amateurs. Gloucestershire did not, in fact, countenance a professional until the following season, when they conscripted W. E. Midwinter, the man who played for both England and Australia.

This was their conquering team: (1) W. G. Grace, captain; (2) E. M. Grace, (3) W. R. Gilbert, (4) F. Townsend, (5) G. F. Grace, (6) W. O. Moberley, (7) T. G. Matthews, (8) C. R. Filgate, (9) R. E. Bush, (10) R. F. Miles and (11) J. A. Bush.

W. G. Grace was the great figure in cricket history and must remain so, but he was never a giant among tiny pygmies. The team of distinguished amateurs whom he led were all sizeable cricketers. E. M. Grace, W. G.'s senior by seven years, was for a short time, before W. G. came to maturity, the most celebrated English cricketer of the period, the first amateur to go on tour to Australia, a punishing bat, a cunning lob bowler, and a fielder at the point of the bat who would have gained the respect, say, of Brian Close. Moreover, most of the stories of W. G.'s supposed gamesmanship are not true and those that have some relation to fact are more rightly attributable to E. M. Both E. M. and W. G. were what we should now call incorrigible 'kidders' and their ceaseless back-chat on the field constituted the family version of exuberant family fun.

All the Graces, father and five sons, were doctors, except G. F. (Fred) who, sad to say, died before his thirtieth birthday and just before qualifying. E. M. was Coroner of Bristol and, like A. N. Hornby of Lancashire, was a fiery little citizen, capable of seizing a barracker by the collar and running him out of the ground. Receiving, while batting at the Oval, a telegram demanding his return to preside over an inquest, he wired back: *Keep corpse on ice till innings declared.* It is a solemn thought that science has now caught up with this request and that E. M. may be hailed as the pioneer of mortuary refrigeration.

Fred was a charming character, less ruthless than his brothers and might even, as W. G. modestly admitted, have developed into the most outstanding cricketer of them all. He is most famous for his part in the first Test match ever played in England, in which he collected a pair, but took the historic catch off what is still reckoned the tallest hit ever made. Bonnor, the big bearded Australian, sent the ball soaring with all his muscular might. Fred ran round with uncanny judgment and waited, taking the catch just as the batsmen were starting their third run. Within a month poor Fred was dead, a victim of congestion of the lungs.

Nearly all the team were all-rounders, most of them quick-footed batsmen, especially W. R. Gilbert, who was a cousin of the Graces and eventually settled in Canada; W. O. Moberley, a rugger international and sports master at Clifton; T. G. Matthews, a tremendous striker of the ball, who once hit a lightning delivery from Yorkshire's fast bowler, Allan Hill, over square-leg, right out of Bramall Lane, and Frank Townsend, head of a famous cricketing family, father of G. L. Townsend, who played with Gloucestershire as a Clifton schoolboy and seemed in turn the best young batsman in England and grandfather of D. C. L. Townsend, who made 193 in the University match in his second year.

As for bowling, the Grace family seldom felt they needed much help with it. Fred with fast medium straight stuff, W. G. with round-arm donkey drops of frequent deadliness and E. M. with his often lethal lobs, could usually account for the enemy. There was, in fact, one match against Yorkshire when W. G. and Fred captured all the wickets. Those who were not bowled or caught and bowled by either were caught by the one off the other. To round off a neat innings victory, out of 314, W. G., Fred and Townsend scored 263, of which W. G.'s share was a modest 167. If by any chance the family needed a little assistance with the ball they could call on R. F. Miles, a left-hander so slow that he could tempt the most cautious batsman to self-destruction. But mostly they managed.

J. A. (Arthur) Bush, the wicket-keeper and W. G.'s best man, went to Australia on W. G.'s 'honeymoon' tour of 1873, and in Gloucestershire's game against Yorkshire at Cheltenham he helped W. G. to add 62 for the last wicket. (W. G. finished with 318 not out.) This culminated the short, bright period in which W. G. made 839 in three innings, once not out. This made his average $419\frac{1}{2}$ and he strongly insisted on the half. It was a month before that he had scored 400 not out against Grimsby and District, an innings which included 4 sixes, 21 fours, 6 threes, 58 twos and 158 singles. The outfield grass was longish, every run was 'run out' and there were 22 fielders. It seems a pity it was not a first class match.

Considering the moderate expectation of life in mid-Victorian times, they were, except for Fred, a long-lived lot. C. R. Filgate, another big hitter, lived to be over 80; T. G. Matthews was riding to hounds at the same age and R. F. Miles, perhaps because slow bowlers suffer less wear and tear, reached 84. R. E. Bush, after thirty years' sheepfarming in Australia, survived into the Second World War and died, at 84, the last of that noble band of brothers. Because I like and admire so many young cricketers of today, I have sworn never to say, 'They don't make 'em like that now.' But there is no law against thinking.

Chapter Six

KENT, 1910

Kent, who have hardly ever failed through the years to produce an attractive side, could almost be called everybody's second favourite. Hang a man, I say, who will not give his first loyalty to his own county, even if it happens to be Blankshire. But there are seventeen counties and it is only natural that there should be, in esteem at least, a recognised second best. Gloucestershire, from Jessop to Hammond, and Sussex, from Ranji to Duleep, are obvious consolation choices. Nobody outside Yorkshire feels sentimental about that county. Life's objective is to beat them and this Yorkshiremen accept as completely just.

But it is only necessary to mention the names of a few Kent cricketers to delineate the people and places that remain in the memory: K. L. Hutchings, Frank Woolley, A. P. F. Chapman, Leslie Ames and Colin Cowdrey. Most of these names come from the days before the big changes, but if a single cricketer had to be picked out as embodying the dash and the joyous attack that we now wistfully associate with 'the true amateur spirit', it would without doubt be Frank Woolley.

It is all the more surprising, then, that Kent have headed the county table only four times and that the last time they did so was well over half a century ago. Their championship victories were in 1906, 1909, 1910 and 1913 and what puzzles me most is why they did not swamp all their rivals in those years of the later 1920s and the earlier 1930s when Woolley and Ames were making 3,000 runs in a season and when

Freeman took 200 wickets eight times in a row, averaging over 260 a summer on all kinds of pitches. Could it be that in the inter-war years the batting was *too* attractive and that soundness was sacrificed to gaiety? Probably not, because between 1919 and 1934 Kent only once came lower than fifth.

The truth remains that in their four pre-1914 victories (a) they achieved a nearly perfect balance between batting and bowling strength; (b) that Blythe, their splendid slow bowler, had more varied and more resourceful backing than the indefatigable Freeman ever had, and (c) that, while there was always a wealth of amateur talent on tap, it could not displace the hard core of indispensable professional batting.

In Kent's four outstanding seasons their results were:

	Played	Won	Lost	Drawn
1906	22	16	2	4
1909	27	16	3	8
1910	25	19	3	3
1913	28	20	3	5

Whichever of these four remarkable seasons we reckon the best, six men – Seymour, Humphreys, Huish, Fairservice, Blythe and Fielder played in all four, and four – Hutchings, Woolley, Dillon and Mason – played in three. Hardinge, also a football international, made regular appearances in 1909 and 1913, and did not leave the game till 1933, when he had 33,519 runs in the book. Woolley, who could not command an unquestioned place in 1906, hit nearly 59,000 runs and took over 2,000 wickets before his retirement in 1938. Blythe, killed in France in 1917, captured 2,506 wickets in his comparatively short career, averaging 170 a season and in 1909, his peak year, taking 215. The deaths of Colin Blythe and K. L. Hutchings in the first war were among cricket's saddest losses, but many of the others have been long-lived. Of these eleven players some are splendidly alive, including Fairservice at 86 and Woolley at 81; Huish lived to 85, Mason to 84 and Hardinge to 79.

It is tempting to choose these fine players as Kent's vintage eleven, with A. P. Day an excellent choice as twelfth man, but, as they never to my knowledge played together as a team, we must look at one of their triumphant summers. Which should it be? In 1906, year of their first championship? This must have been a superb side, if only because they could not find a regular place for 'the colt' Woolley. They fought out the championship with Yorkshire literally to the last single, because it fell to them at the last moment when Gloucestershire beat Yorkshire by one run. But could there BE a vintage Kent eleven without Frank Woolley? It would be a contradiction in terms.

In 1906 the Australians came over, brought bad weather with them and almost contemptuously defeated England in the rubber. Kent led the county field until in Tonbridge week they suffered two swingeing defeats and had to fight their way out of the rough. This they achieved, starting with a crushing victory by an innings and 300 runs. From then on, they never lost another match, winning most of their remaining victories by an innings. Mason and Day ended the season at the top of the batting and, with Rhodes now going in first for England, Blythe was easily the best bowler in the kingdom.

The next year success was repeated with centuries in quantity from Hutchings, Seymour and Humphreys, penetrative bowling by Woolley (134 wickets) and Blythe (175) and the second appearance of D. W. Carr, the googly-teaching school-master. Lastly, after running second in 1911 and third in 1912, Kent rose again with a conquering effort in 1913. This side did not differ much from its distinguished predecessors, but it had the distinction of winning one more victory than any of them. Which of the four shall we choose?

If we discard 1906 we shall miss out C. J. Burnup, a graceful Malvernian batsman who hit 21 hundreds for Kent, was a *Wisden* Cricketer of the Year and lived till he was 84.

Without 1909 we should miss the astonishing debut of D. W. Carr at the age of 37 and without 1910 we should lose F. H. Knott, the batsman who came in straight from Tonbridge School and scored a century in his third county game. Finally, if we do without 1913, we not only do without Jack Hubble, who succeeded Fred Huish as wicket-keeper and made over 10,000 runs; we must also do without K. L. Hutchings, who remains, next to Woolley, Kent's most dazzling batsman.

On the whole, then, after agonising reappraisal and a lot of running round in circles, I would settle for 1910, which embodies our key figures and allows us to have either F. H. Knott or D. W. Carr, according to the state of the wicket, as twelfth man. This tremendous eleven would comprise: E. W. Dillon (captain), James Seymour, E. Humphreys, K. L. Hutchings, F. E. Woolley, F. R. Mason, F. H. Knott, F. H. Huish, W. J. Fairservice, C. Blythe and A. Fielder, with D. W. Carr, waiting in the wings

It is late in the day to praise any of them individually. E. W. Dillon, who shrewdly captained Kent from 1909 to 1913, thus including three of their four championships under his leadership, was a batsman capable of defending firmly at need, but also of going more cheerfully for the runs. Seymour and 'Punter' Humphreys were (with Hardinge at a later date) the side's indispensable batting backbone. Through this decade of all the talents, talented amateurs would brighten August with their blazers, some professionals might have to accept temporary redundancy, but Seymour, a most attractive off-side player, and Humphreys, a natural bad-wicket batsman, never suffered this indignity. Both were prolific scorers in county games, Seymour getting his 1,000 a year seventeen times and Humphreys seven.

Cricket has scope for manifold gifts: some are brave defenders; some are greedy acquisitors; some leave a name for sheer splendour. Among this rare band were K. S. Ranjitsinhji, Victor Trumper and, during a short career, K. L. Hutchings. Few batsmen have cast a magic spell in this or any other age, but testimony to the glory that was Hutchings is universal. In 1906, the unsentimental *Wisden* called him 'the sensation of the season, the English Trumper.' Only Trumper, in fact, ever drove good bowling on both sides of the wicket with such effortless ease. Hutchings' power was in his wrists and forearms. It was sad that an athlete of such steely strength should suffer from imperfect health; he toured Australia with A. O. Jones's unlucky team in 1907–08, but after one blazing century, his health let him down and, though he played with Kent till 1912, he never quite reached his gleaming peak again. There has been nobody in recent years capable of recalling the power and elegance of Hutchings, except P. B. H. May at his noblest and E. R. Dexter, as in his unforgettable innings, lived at Lord's in 1963 against the fury of Hall and Griffith.

I have been told of a present-day young England player who innocently asked: 'Was Woolley really good?' May heaven, in its infinite mercy, forgive him. I am grudging in the use of the word 'great', but if Woolley does not merit it, who, but two or three, can? It is not his 59,000 runs and 2,000 wickets, though only Grace, Rhodes and Hirst approach that class; it is not his 145 hundreds or even his 95 and 93 against Gregory and McDonald in 1921. What made him supreme was the serene beauty of his every stroke, so that to think of Kent is compellingly to think of Woolley.

The solid professional core which kept out some of the holiday amateurs could not keep out J. R. Mason, an all-rounder who toured Australia with Stoddart's second team, was one of the 14 from whom the 1902 Birmingham team, England's greatest eleven, was chosen, and once, batting with W. G., ran the Old Man out by lapping him with accidental disrespect. He was an upright forward-playing batsman and a medium-fast bowler who could nip them up off the pitch.

The last four on the score-card scarcely varied between the first championship and the first war. These were the wicket-keeper, Huish, on whom, as *Wisden* said, 'time had no effect,' and the three bowlers, Fairservice (medium), Blythe (slow), and Fielder (pretty fast). They formed a trio almost as formidable as Yorkshire's Haigh, Rhodes and Hirst. Blythe was the greatest of all English slow bowlers, always excepting Rhodes – Ranji thought Blythe even subtler – and by 1910 Rhodes was an England opening batsman. Fielder, though not quite a Larwood or a McDonald, was in the finest tradition of county fast bowlers. He had two finest hours. In the first innings of the 1906 Gentlemen v. Players match he took all ten wickets. ('Did you really take all ten, Arthur?' 'I did that, and eight of 'em was out.') His other feat was his share (112 not out) in 1909 with Woolley (175) of Kent's, and indeed any county's, record last-wicket stand of 235. As he grew older he tended to frown on what he thought the effeteness of the younger professionals. 'Too many sweaters,' he would growl; 'too much ginger pop and not enough good ale.'

I believe this Kent team of 1910, or in fact any of the other three, could, by benefit of H. G. Wells's time machine, beat any team except the best of Yorkshire or Surrey. Finally, there were good hopes that the team of 1967, eager, youthful and inspiringly led, might have secured Kent's fifth championship. In the event they lost by a head. But in the future who knows?

Chapter Seven

LANCASHIRE, 1928

Lancashire's experience in recent seasons of life among the lowly has naturally caused distress in the County Palatine. It should be no reason for gratification anywhere else. There is truth in the old belief that, when the north is strong, England is strong; there is also sad truth in the converse.

My nobler namesake did well to sing of his Hornby and his Barlow long ago. When Lancashire took the county championship in 1897 Barlow had turned to umpiring and that fiery particle, A. N. Hornby, still captain at 50, was batting lower down the order. Nevertheless, they could present their country with such outstanding names as the young A. C. MacLaren, Albert Ward (a Yorkshire-born opening bat with seven England caps), J. T. Tyldesley, one of cricket's immortals with strong claims to a place in an all-time world eleven; Johnny Briggs (33 caps), also with cosmic claims, perhaps, leaving out W. G., the most exciting all-rounder between Alfred Mynn and George Hirst; Frank Sugg and Willis Cuttell (two caps each) and Arthur Mold (three caps), a daunting fast bowler.

My step-Uncle Walter, a shrewd assessor of relative merits between the 1890s and the mid 1930s, and with all the Yorkshireman's respect for the traditional foe, would have none of the 1897 lot. He maintained that too many of them were Yorkshiremen, anyhow; that Mold, their demon bowler, was either the best bowler in England or the worst chucker in the world; and that the best of them, MacLaren, Tyldesley and Cuttell, were all more mature in Lancashire's championship-winning team of 1904. Let me set down this formidable eleven: (1) A. C. MacLaren, captain, (2) R. H. Spooner, (3) J. T. Tyldesley, (4) the Australian doctor, L. O. S. Poidevin, (5) James Hallows, uncle of the more famous Charles, (6) A. H. Hornby, son of A. N., (7) the Everton and England footballer, Jack Sharp, (8) W. R. Cuttell, (9) fast, off-spinning Australian, Alec Kermode, (10) competent wicket-keeper, Charlie Smith, and (11) the ineffable Walter Brearley. In any event, Uncle Walter would argue any Lancashire that left out Spooner, England's most 'beautiful' batsman and Brearley, England's most truculent bowler, was not the Lancashire for his money. 'We'd beat 'em too easy,' was his last word.

But Uncle Walter has long departed and I only saw that team as a lad of ten. Most of my Lancashire acquaintances have no doubt that their vintage eleven was one of the three that, under the wise leadership of Major Leonard Green, marched to successive victories in 1926, 1927 and 1928. They slipped to second place in 1929, but returned in triumph to the top in 1930 under the gallant Peter Eckersley, killed ten years later in the Second World War. Who would be so bold as to choose between these four? Most of my Lancashire friends would, anyway.

One salient fact makes the choice easier and, at the same time, harder: easier because the same eight players formed the backbone of all four elevens and two more played in three; harder, perhaps, because there is always a difference of opinion about the odd man. The spinal links of this splendid column were Charles Hallows, Ernest Tyldesley, Frank Watson, Jack Iddon, F. M. Sibbles, Richard Tyldesley, E. A. (Ted) McDonald, and George Duckworth. No county, except Yorkshire in the 1920s and Surrey in the 1950s, has ever in successive seasons had so hard a core.

Take bowling first, as in the north you always should. Summer after summer McDonald and Dick Tyldesley bore the burden and heat of the day. McDonald, who in 1921 had come over with Armstrong's conquering Australians and, with

NOTTINGHAMSHIRE, 1929.
Left: George Gunn, one of English cricket's greatest characters. *Below:* Was this County cricket's finest opening attack? Harold Larwood (*left*) and Bill Voce

SOMERSET, 1966. *Above:* The 1966 team. *Back row (l. to r.):* P. Robinson, G. Clayton, A. Clarkson, F. Rumsey, R. Palmer, M. Kitchen, R. Virgin. *Front row:* G. Atkinson, B. Langford, C. R. M. Atkinson (captain), W. Alley, K. Palmer. *Below left:* Bill Alley, the great Australian all-rounder. *Below right:* Fred Rumsey at full stretch

Jack Gregory as his partner, had torn England's batting to tatters, joined Lancashire in 1924 and brought to their attack a deadly blend of pace and fire. People still disagree as to whether he or Larwood or Lindwall was the finest of all fast bowlers. I am not sure. I never saw Tom Richardson. Just as McDonald was the master of controlled fury, so Dick Tyldesley was the master of guile, amiably offering his insidious off-breaks. He got many wickets with deliveries that played clever tricks and many more with balls whose clever trick was to play no tricks at all.

In these four glorious seasons their tale of captures in all first class matches was prodigious:

	1926	1927	1928	1930	Total
McDonald	175	150	190	108	623
R. Tyldesley	128	100	104	140	472

Even such eminent practitioners in destruction needed assistant destroyers. Their helpers included Jack Iddon, who bowled left-hand slow and batted right, pretty fast. In the 1930s he was one of the country's liveliest all-rounders. Yorkshire will not quickly forget his nine for 42 in the 1937 Roses match at Bramall Lane. Like McDonald, he was killed in the Third World War, the war of the motor car against the human race. The other bowler of note was F. M. Sibbles, a tireless worker who thought nothing of getting Hobbs out twice in one match, and who each season advanced steadily as an off-spinner.

The batting foundation in all four sides was laid by Ernest Tyldesley, Charles Hallows and Frank Watson, with help in three of the teams by that most rocklike of batsmen, Harry Makepeace. Uncle Walter would not have deemed this quartet as impressive as the giants of 1904, but his team, eminent though they were, only came out on top once. About the batsmen of 1926 to 1930 there was a businesslike professionalism with a touch of near-genius in one of them. Ernest Tyldesley was the younger brother of J. T. — there were sixteen years between them – and the other Tyldesleys, produced by Lancashire in such numbers, were no relations.

In assessing the brothers you will find a similarity in their records. Both scored about 38,000 runs, and about 100 centuries, with Ernest slightly ahead in both instances. I am prejudiced, having watched J. T. play a superb not out century to save Lancashire in the first Roses match I ever saw, but anyone who saw cricket in the 1920s and 1930s would be dull of soul if he did not admire the noble gifts of Ernest Tyldesley. If you lived in the batting era of Hobbs, Sutcliffe, Hammond, Hendren, Woolley and Jardine, England caps were not easy to come by, but Ernest wore fourteen with distinction. If Johnny wore more than twice as many, the answer was simple: for the key position of No. 3 Ernest was challenged by Walter Hammond. Johnny, even in the golden age of amateur batting, was challenged by nobody. Even so, Ernest was the finest Lancashire batsman of his era, free, elegant, unruffled, consistent as C. B. Fry was once consistent; in 1926 he hit ten hundreds, four of them in a row and in 1928 his hundreds were also ten and his aggregate over 3,000. Such difference as there was between the brothers lay in the intangible contrast between genius and the highest talent.

Charles Hallows was another of his county's most prolific scorers. For many years he was a partner in a solid opening pair; first with Makepeace, then with Watson. His richest season was 1928 when, like only two other batsmen in history, he scored 1,000 runs in May. (Three others, Grace, Hammond and Bradman, twice, have scored 1,000 before June, but that is not quite the same thing.) There was no holding back his left-handed flow, modified as it was by concentration and reliability. At times concentration overcame his natural appetite and his tempo was adagio rather than allegretto, but in Major Green's three summers his average went from 31 to 75 and 64.

The legend of Harry Makepeace varies geographically. Outside Lancashire he is credited with the 'no fours before lunch' story in Roses matches and with thinking discretion so much the better part of valour that valour, at any rate before lunch, was in itself discreditable. Lancashire folk, if they do not know you well, will strenuously deny all this; if you are admitted to their close friendship, they will tell you even more historic tales of Harry's canniness. All the same, the real Makepeace story rests on his strong belief that, if your defence wasn't 100 per cent sound, you wouldn't make a batsman in 100 years. I know two great Yorkshiremen, Wilfred Rhodes and Sir Leonard Hutton, who believe the same thing.

Frank Watson (all four teams) was his imperturbable partner. The bright-eyed rebel against these principles was Eddie Paynter, who came into the 1930 eleven. His attitude was simple. When told that his habit of knocking the cover off the ball would shock Old Trafford spectators, he replied: 'I can't pander to that lot.'

The other chunk of hard core was George Duckworth, the England wicket-keeper, probably the liveliest character of them all. With an appeal like the crack of doom he 'kept' with equanimity to McDonald's flyers and Dick Tyldesley's floaters and, when he went to keep for England, his place was taken by that other remarkable character, Bill Farrimond, who would every now and then change places with Duckworth in the reverse order so that, if asked by the unwary whom he played for would reply, poker-faced: 'Oh, Lancashire seconds and England.'

These then were the backbone men. The player who, besides Makepeace, graced three of the four elevens, was Major Leonard Green, a firm but tactful disciplinarian, an eager field, and a much better bat than most amateur captains were given credit for at the time. By the flexible strength of his personality he welded a collection of tough individualists into a formidable fighting machine.

The 1930 captain, killed alas in the Second World War, was Peter Eckersley, whom I would set down as twelfth man in 1926, a lively batsman in 1928, and an inspiring captain in 1930.

The respective merits of the four elevens remain matters of opinion. A friend of mine, once president of the county club, will have nobody but the lads of 1926, and for one reason only: they included the ingenious, humorous, delightfully exasperating Cecil Parkin. I have seen him baffle a whole batting side into impotence; I have also seen him pretend to take catches when the ball was at the boundary and his chief delight in running between wickets was to lap his partner. If entertainment was the sole aim of cricket, then Parkin was the game's chief comedian, but I think, and I hope the thought is not treasonable, that his impish fun prevented him from reaching the austere heights of a Rhodes, a Blythe or a Grimmett. In any event, he played in only half the side's 1926 matches.

The 1926 team lost two matches, the 1927 team lost only one. The only difference was that Eckersley, a vigorous young batsman, held the place made vacant by Parkin's departure. He was absent from the 1928 team, but his place was filled by that very lively all-rounder, Len Hopwood, who made the post his own, held it in the 1930 team, did the double twice and gained two England caps against Australia in 1934. He might well have had more. The 1930 team had lost Green, but Eckersley moved in as its happy and successful captain.

Each side had its merits and still has its enthusiasts. If I have to make a choice, free from selector's responsibilities, I would vote for the 1928 combination. They came to their third successive triumph under a splendid leader; they did not lose a single match; of their dozen draws, nine were firmly in their favour. Give me 1928 every time. And may I reply at once to those who tell me that in 1950 Lancashire tied for first place with a powerful Surrey by saying that a side containing Tattersall, Statham, Ikin and Washbrook was rather a good one. Finally, let nobody, least of all any Yorkshireman, gloat over Lancashire's current misfortune. Lancashire's return to strength will be good for us all.

Chapter Eight

LEICESTERSHIRE, 1967

Leicestershire is, par excellence, the hunting county and its cricketing badge is the running fox. Its cricketers have hunted the county championship since (let us say, not to start an argument) 1894 and they have gone gallantly at their fences, sometimes clearing them and often coming down at them. They have been near the bottom of the table oftener than they have been near the top, but they have produced many fine cricketers from A. D. Pougher (pronounced Puffer), who once took five Australian wickets for none to Maurice Hallam who, with 22,749 runs in the book, is still going strong. They have also bred characters worthy to ride with Mr Jorrocks, such as the gifted fast bowler, Alec Skelding, who told me with a straight face that when the county sacked him because he wore spectacles, the only job open to him was that of first class umpire, a post which he filled with dignity and distinction for several seasons.

There are renowned Leicestershire cricketers whose names are household words, but who were never members of outstanding county sides. Astill and Geary were probably the most talented pair of county all-rounders since Hirst and Rhodes, but they were tremendous individual members of teams seldom near the top of the table. The Leicestershire I first saw as a boy sixty years ago was stuffed with rich characters, but I did not understand character then. 'To such poor advantage (in *Wisden's* stately phrase) did they appear,' that a boy might be forgiven for seeing only the merits of his own county, and not the brave struggles of their foes. Brave, yes, but vain. George Hirst, who, as Uncle Walter, Lord Hawke and I agreed, was the greatest county cricketer who ever lived, took eight wickets for 25 in the first innings and then, after Yorkshire had scored a mere 114, took seven, all clean bowled, for 38 in the second. Yorkshire needed only one run to win and, although the match was over by half past twelve on the second day, few Yorkshiremen in the crowd actually demanded their money back.

This slaughter by our hero prevented me from realising how good his victims were, but Uncle Walter, always the soul of objectivity once Yorkshire had safely won, told me some things about the best of them. Albert Knight, though he had been a 'leg' of Hirst's hat-trick, was an England bat of the sturdiest kind and a Methodist local preacher who had written a book called *The Complete Cricketer,* which blended sound technique with pulpit eloquence. J. H. King, one of the 'nubbly' left-handers of the period, once scored two hundreds for Players against Gentlemen after having been brought in as reserve. He was also, though a slow left-hander, to find himself picked for a Test two years later as the toughest opening bowler England had got. There was Sam Coe, another loamy left-hander and V. F. S. (Vivian) Crawford, a mighty hitter and the eldest of a clerico-cricketing family of which J. N., the youngest was the most famous. There was W. W. Odell, who bowled almost as fast as Hirst and in this match took eight for 40, and their No. 11, Ewart Astill a lad of 19, just starting a splendid career. Uncle Walter could not, of course, tell me of the celebrated feat of C. J. B. Wood, because it did not happen till four years later, when at Bradford he went in first on the first day, scored 107 and 117, both not out, and remained in the field all three days, Yorkshiremen, to coin a phrase, had grown accustomed to his face . . .

If this seems an astonishing feat, it looks ordinary beside some of the doings of a later opening batsman, Maurice Hallam, who in 1959, admittedly a batsman's year, scored 210 not out and 157 against Glamorgan at Leicester; two years later he made 203 and 143 against Sussex and four years later still 107 and 149 against Worcestershire. There was a Bradmanesque touch about such batting.

I pick out Hallam, over the years Leicestershire's most prolific scorer, except Leslie Berry, because he was one of the 1953 side, captained by Charles Palmer. This team ran third in the championship and was acclaimed as the county's most successful eleven so far. But for one fact they would have been my vintage selection, despite the absence of such big names as Wood, Knight, King, Sam Coe, Astill, Uncle George Geary and all. They were: (1) G. Lester, (2) M. R. Hallam, (3) M. Tompkin, (4) C. H. Palmer, captain, (5) V. E. Jackson, (6) G. A. Smithson, (7) V. S. Munden, (8) F. E. Walsh, (9) J. Firth, (10) J. Goodwin, (11) C. T. Spencer. They were a splendidly combative side, with a leader whose modesty was as striking as his gifts. (When he took eight for seven against the champion county – it should have been eight for none, but for a missed catch – he went into their dressing room and apologised profoundly.) Under his leadership Leicestershire lost seven games, but never lost by poverty of spirit. Twice they came from a long way behind to bring off exciting wins, and their victory over Yorkshire by six runs caused palpitations all round the ground as, in a whirlwind climax Trueman, who had already hit four fours, was unfraternally stumped by Firth, his fellow-Yorkshireman. And what Freddie said to Jackie marked an interesting advance in English semantics.

They were a team of all the talents. Maurice Tompkin, who, alas, died young, was that season only a handful of runs short of 2,000 and Palmer, who also headed the county bowling, scored well over 1,600. Hallam and Smithson were eager and attractive bats, with Lester as solid support, while the heavier bowling was in the hands of two hard-headed Australians, Vic Jackson, who bowled off-breaks, and Walsh, who took 102 wickets with left-hand spin. Goodwin, a fast-medium left-hander, shared the faster stuff with Spencer, who that year had a Test trial. They never slackened, even though their younger players were often either just going into or coming out of National Service. By August they were at the top of the table, along with the lordly Surrey, and finished up third with Lancashire.

This eleven, I repeat, would have been my favourite, if it had not been for the team that in 1967, under the captaincy of G. A. R. Lock, challenged the highest and, after a breathless last fortnight, ended equal second with Kent, whom many people, in any event, thought the season's best.

This Leicestershire contained two who had been likely lads in the team of fourteen years before: one was Hallam, who had led the side for two years but had ceded the captaincy to Lock in 1966; the other was Terry Spencer who, at the age of 36, was bowling with all his old stingo. The team was: (1) M. R. Hallam, (2) M. E. Norman, (3) B. J. Booth, (4) P. Marner, (5) C. C. Inman, (6) B. Dudleston, (7) J. Birkenshaw, (8) R. Tolchard, (9) G. A. R. Lock, captain, (10) C. T. Spencer and (11) J. Cotton.

Looking down the card, it is hard to find a weak spot. Five batsmen – Norman, Hallam, Booth, Inman and Marner – scored over 1,000 runs, four of them over 1,400, and eight had averages of over 20. Bowling was varied, with speed in the hands of Cotton and Spencer, Birkenshaw having his best season with the ball and, with the bat, falling only a little short of his first double. Lock, with 128, took his 100 wickets for the fourteenth time, while, if batsmen were obdurate, there was always Marner to take the odd wickets.

Hallam, relieved of the cares of captaincy, batted as attractively as ever, finding a solid partner in M. E. J. (Mick) Norman a blond but hardly a bombshell. Nevertheless, he was the county's highest scorer and enjoyed his best season since transferring from his native Northamptonshire. Brian Booth, late of Lancashire, also had a good year; though not as aggressive as Marner, he is harder to get out.

I know people who would sooner see Clive Inman in

full flow than any other batsman you could name. This left-hander from Ceylon has wrists as strong as steel and flexible as whipcord and, when you see him launch a square-cut, you would wonder the ball didn't catch fire. I am less impressed by his record of scoring 51 in eight minutes against Nottinghamshire, including 32 off one over from Norman Hill. Now Norman is a good soul and a high-scoring bat, but hardly my idea of a demon bowler, and I would rather watch Inman slaughtering a fierce, fast attack. That is the time when the sparks fly in earnest. Visitors to Grace Road would rather see, say, Hallam and Inman or Inman and Marner in partnership than Norman and Booth, but all true batsmen have their value and we cannot have colour television all the time. True batsmen include Barry Dudleston, a young batsman from Stockport who in his first qualified year has made a promising start.

I first saw Jackie Birkenshaw as a schoolboy, playing for Yorkshire's Federation team. I next saw his first first class game, in which he sorely puzzled Sussex's leading batsmen. That was nine years ago and for three seasons he played well, but not quite well enough to establish himself in Yorkshire, a particularly demanding county. Specially registered for Leicestershire, he has had good times and bad, sometimes of bad health, and 1967 has been his first truly tip-top season. He is a stubborn but not necessarily slow left-hand bat; and eager close fielder and a puzzling right-hand off-break bowler whose action involves a high jump, so that his front foot comes down hard and the off-break lifts, often awkwardly. Few things give me warmer pleasure than the sight of a gifted youngster who has come through hard times to success.

Leicestershire have been lucky in finding a young wicket-keeper-batsman, educated at so classic a cricket school as Malvern. Roger Tolchard kept wicket for Devonshire when seventeen and for Hampshire 2nd eleven at eighteen. Since then he has developed into what seems, always excepting Alan Knott, the quickest young wicket-keeper in the country. Thirty-six is not the ideal age for a fast bowler, but Terry Spencer, when joined by John Cotton, who came over from Nottinghamshire in 1965, has helped to form a happily hostile partnership. Few opening pairs are more respected.

That leaves us with Graham Anthony Richard Lock, one of the most remarkable cricketers of our time. His earlier county and Test career covered the long ascendancy of Surrey and the bright, if transient, post-war period when England were on top of the world. His records are prodigious. 47 Test caps, 2627 wickets up to the end of the season, and nearly 800 catches. (Only Woolley and W. G. have caught more.) In 1962–63 he emigrated to play for Western Australia and has since spent the English winters there; joined Leicestershire in 1965; as captain, bumped them up six places in 1966, and brought them to shared second in 1967. His first Test was against India in 1952 and his last, so far, against West Indies in 1963. Whether he was specifically invited to tour the West Indies in 1968 I do not know. I only know that at the time of the initial invitation the sports desk of my newspaper rang me up in the middle of the night, demanding confirmation of the rumour, and when I asked him in the Leicestershire dressing-room at a more civilised hour, his reply was as enigmatic as his 'wrong 'un'. But everybody admits the selectors might have done worse . . .

Records, however imposing, do not display his vividness as a cricket character. No slow bowler ever looked so hostile, no fielder ever menaced the batsman so balefully. For nearly 20 years he has been the game's most colourful showman and I do not forget Godfrey Evans. I use the word in no pejorative sense; anyone who could regard Tony Lock as a *mere* show-off would be a mere silly. The fact is: he encourages and galvanises his colleagues with his *verve, élan* and *panache,* and all those glittering French words for which we have no equivalent in the American the English now speak. He has been the most consistently brilliant fielder we have ever had. Is it a fault that his catches often look brilliant?

When one of his side takes a difficult catch or captures a difficult wicket, he tends to congratulate the performer with an effusion of the type normally seen, say, at Craven Cottage. True, but the rumour that catches are sometimes dropped from sheer terror of such congratulations can be discounted. Admittedly, Lord Hawke would not so have embraced Boffy Peel or Ted Wainwright, but . . . other times, other manners, and manners based on bubbling enthusiasm are not bad manners. The proof of the pudding is in the success that Lock's exuberant leadership has brought. Not that Leicestershire are a one-man team; that would be unjust to ten fine cricketers. It is just that those ten play all the better for the zeal and zest of the one man.

Chapter Nine

MIDDLESEX, 1947

Middlesex have won the county championship five times and have had some outstanding players in teams that won no championships at all, but I have little doubt that the ultimate choice of a vintage eleven lies between the winning team of Sir Pelham Warner's last season (1920) and the side of 1947, that summer – do you remember? – when Compton, Edrich and the sun all shone, in glorious combination.

Besides these two peaks, old folk recall 1903, the season that sent Warner on his triumphant tour of Australia in 1903–04; there was also 1921, when F. T. Mann, taking over from 'Plum', carried on the good work. There was also the little matter of 1866, when Middlesex were borne aloft on the shoulders of Tom Hearne and a covey of Walkers. Aged as I am, I do not remember this, nor, come to that, did my Uncle Walter. He did tell me, however, about the victorious Middlesex of 1903, captained by Gregor MacGregor, who lost only one match. This was to Yorkshire at Bradford, and Uncle Walter saw every ball of it. Hirst and Rhodes took eight wickets each and Haigh had the other four. The old man had no animosity against the visitors, except that, as he said, they had too many foreigners, such as MacGregor from Scotland; Albert Trott, from Australia; and Jack Rawlin, a renegade Yorkshireman from Greaseborough, near Rotherham. If the word *quisling* had been invented in the life-time of either of them, that is what Uncle Walter would have called honest Jack.

That leaves 1920 (or 1921, when the results and the players,

except that Warner had departed, were not so very different)
to compete with 1947. If I choose 1947, it is not so much
that it was vastly superior. It's chief excellence was its richness
in the things for which we vainly sigh today.

Not that I could dismiss 1920 without a pang; it had an
excellent fast bowler, named Durston; it had its characters
and it had its twins. If the twins happened to be among the
most eminent cricketers of the century, that remains always
to the credit of Middlesex. The huge scores of Compton and
Edrich in 1947 are known and admired and are not so far
from the present day that they have faded into the incredibility
gap. But 1920 also had its scores and its twins to make them.
Think of an odd figure or two in their totals against Warwickshire and Sussex in their first two county games:

Mr P. F. Warner retired hurt	76
H. W. Lee st. Smith b Hands	102
J. W. Hearne	96
E. Hendren	158
Mr P. F. Warner c Street b Gilligan	139
H. W. Lee c Roberts b Gilligan	119
J. W. Hearne not out	116
Mr N. Haig c H. L. Wilson b Tate	131

I count myself twice lucky to have watched Hendren and
'young' Jack Hearne as well as Compton and Edrich.

I saw the 1920 side's last match at Lord's. Owing to a
beautiful bat-carrying 167 by Sandham, they found themselves
73 behind. They pulled the game round, however, and in the
fourth innings young Greville Stevens bowled so destructively
that they won by 55 runs at twenty past six. A crowd of
25,000 ran amok. Plum Warner, the retiring captain, was
carried off shoulder high, waving his Harlequin cap, to such
peril of life and limb that it is still a wonder to me that
he survived (a) to make a breathlessly inaudible speech from
the balcony and (b) lived another 40-odd happy and useful

years longer. His companions on that August evening were: (1) C. H. L. Skeet, (2) H. W. Lee, (3) J. W. Hearne, (4) E. Hendren, (6) F. T. Mann, (7) N. Haig, (8) G. T. S. Stevens, (9) H. K. Longman, (10) H. R. Murrell and (11) F. J. Durston. I might have been inclined to replace H. K. Longman by Dr C. H. Gunesekara, an excellent all-rounder, with a lofty backlift, from Ceylon, but the change could have made little difference.

If we reckon that the 1947 side was even better, we might as well set down their names for a start: (1) J. D. Robertson, (2) S. M. Brown, (3) W. J. Edrich, (4) D. C. S. Compton, (5) F. G. Mann, (6) R. W. V. Robins, captain, (7) A. Thompson, (8) L. H. Compton, (9) J. Sims, (10) J. A. Young and (11) L. Gray. Look at those first four names; it is hard to find a quartet like them. True, nineteen years before England could start with Hobbs, Sutcliffe, Hammond and Jardine, while on Bradman's first meteoric visit here, he could confront us with Woodfull, Ponsford, himself and McCabe. But here was a mere county side that could start with four men who in the season hit well over 12,000 runs between them. Fantastic? You have only to recall some of the batting you have seen of late at Lord's to realise how fantastic it was.

Jack Robertson may have been slightly overshadowed by the sheer magnificence of Compton, but a batsman who made 2,760 in the season could afford to smile at shadows. He was during the whole of his career one of the two or three most polished batsmen in the country. In that career, which brought him nearly 32,000 runs, I doubt if a single one of them came from an ugly stroke. As a batsman (and a person) he was incapable of ill manners. He was a model cricketer in the sense that you could with perfect confidence take your small nephew to see him and say: 'Watch this man. The way he makes his strokes is exactly the right way to make them.' His opening partner, Sid Brown, was less elegant, but of high value; when you saw him make a hook or a square-cut, it was as though he wielded a blacksmith's hammer and you wondered why the sparks didn't fly.

With respect, I should never have urged my nephew to watch Edrich and Compton with the counsel: 'Learn to bat like that, my boy.' It would have been cruelty to children. They were both inspired, especially in that season, by qualities that could not be taught. Edrich had an explosive exuberance and Compton an elusive magic that were intensely individual and to tell the young to imitate either would have been like telling a green young political candidate: 'Go in and act like Churchill, that's all you have to do!' The well-loved 'Robinson Crusoe' said of them: 'They go together in English cricket, as Gilbert and Sullivan go together in English opera,' and he made the point that, while none of the four was the greatest in his own line of territory, as pairs they were unrivalled in the art of giving pleasure to English audiences.

Though Compton and Edrich scored colossally, they achieved something more than gigantic totals. They set about the bowling from the word Go, as though every ball could be scored off, by Edrich in his brusque, impatient way, as though bowlers were men of no substance, anyhow; and by Compton through some secret enchantment of his own, as though he had set the copy book strokes to music. He seemed to caress rather than batter the ball to the boundary and, by the time he reached one of his 18 centuries, he looked as though he could just as easily have used a fountain pen as a bat.

Pick up a couple of score-cards:

Middlesex

S. M. Brown retired hurt	13
J. D. Robertson c Watson b Walsh	75
W. J. Edrich c Riddington b Sperry	257
D. C. S. Compton st Corrall b Walsh	151

England

L. Hutton b Rowan	18
C. Washbrook c Tuckett b Dawson	65
W. J. Edrich b Mann	189
D. C. S. Compton c Rowan b Tuckett	208

You may wonder why Middlesex needed more than four batsmen, but there were good men to follow: F. G. (George) Mann, who eighteen months later was to lead a winning MCC side in South Africa, and R. W. V. Robins, whose name was synonymous with eagerness and dash, a furious batsman, an England slow bowler, the best cover-point between Hobbs and Washbrook, and a leader with a true flair for victory.

Nor did the departure of these six reveal a tail. Thompson, a stubborn and resourceful No. 7, stood in the breach more than once when Compton, Edrich and sometimes Robertson were called to higher duty. Leslie Compton, a big, burly figure, as befitted an Arsenal centre-half, perhaps lacked as a wicket-keeper the conjuror's sleight of hand of, say, a Strudwick or an Alan Knott, but he performed with deceptive efficiency behind the stumps and was capable of the occasional century at need. This leaves us with three bowlers, Young, Sims and Gray, all links in the victory chain and all characters in their own right.

There are some who, dazzled by the twins' brilliance, have described this eleven as a county who topped the table on batting alone. Normally bowling is the vital factor, as with Surrey in the lordly 1950s and with Yorkshire in any decade, but to dismiss Middlesex '47 as a team without bowling is to imagine a vain thing. In the season Young took 159 wickets, Sims 124, and Gray 98. And do not forget that Edrich, as fast as anybody in England in his opening overs, took 67, while Compton bowled left-handed chinamen and googlies which amused him as much as they exasperated the 73 batsmen they lured to their doom.

SURREY, 1955. *Above:* Two all time greats: Alec Bedser (*left*) and Peter May.
Below: The 1955 team at the Oval: *Back row (l. to r.):* R. Pratt, D. Cox,
P. Loader, T. Clark, G. Lock, D. Fletcher, K. Barrington, M. Willett,
B. Constable. *Front row:* M. Stewart, E. A. Bedser, A. McIntyre, P. May,
Stuart Surridge (Captain), A. V. Bedser, J. Laker, R. Swetman

Sussex, 1932. Two great Sussex all-rounders: James Langridge (*left*), and Maurice Tate who took 160 wickets in 1932. *Below:* K. S. Duleepsinjhi, here seen batting against the Australians in 1930. 'Duleep' hit 5 centuries in 1932, with an average of 52

Young was a delightful person, except to his victims: small, dapper, with a comedian's mobile face – his father was a celebrated comic – and his slow left-hand deliveries had immaculate length and bewildering spin. Sims was for years one of England's problem bowlers. A poker-faced humourist, when facing him you never knew what his googlies were going to do and his friends, in chorus, would whisper: 'Neither does Jim.' Which was a pretty good joke because to take 129 wickets without a notion of what you were playing at was surely the work of a master mind.

Some of his sayings are collectors' pieces. In an earlier period Hendren, his batting partner, accused him of backing away from a fast bowler, possibly Larwood or Constantine.

Hendren (*sternly*): 'Stop kicking the square-leg umpire. You scared or something?'

Sims (*blandly*): 'Not at all. Just a trifle apprehensive.'

And it was Jim who suffered what is the bowler's nightmare, three successive balls that shaved the lucky batsman's stumps, a fate which would have driven the average bowler to torrential profanity. Jim, on the contrary, turned to his captain with a winning smile.

'Remarkable, Mr Robins,' he murmured equably and, just as equably, finished the over. When he did the hat-trick against South Africa nobody thought it remarkable.

Mr Gray is now a respected first class umpire; in 1947 he was a model fast bowler, always willing, always a trier, always dedicated to the task of dismissing batsmen on pitches which in themselves seemed dedicated to the job of relieving batsmen of all anxieties. That on such pitches he should bowl nearly 1,000 overs was highly to his credit. It was typical of his atrocious luck that he should miss his hundred wickets by no more than the odd couple. Had he attended the Scarborough Festival, along with Young and Brown, those two wickets would have been handed him on a plate, as a matter of right, with parsley round them.

When all is said, we come back to the team, because, as

Gertrude Stein might have said, a team is a team is a team: a swift, smooth machine, built of consummate components and guided by an operator, that is, a captain, whose chief characteristic was an overmastering energy. Any player under Walter Robins who did not share Walter Robins's enthusiasm for three days at a time at the least would probably have sunk in his tracks and died of shame.

I do not believe, though I could be wrong, that in any year any county made more runs than did Middlesex in 1947, but this alone would not have brought a string of victories, because the size of your score must be strictly measured against your ability to get the enemy out twice in three days. This objective they splendidly achieved by batting at full gallop so that their bowlers could deal faithfully with the foe at their leisure. Ideally, they would win the toss, declare at 400 for four, three (or possibly two) and then give their opponents a hellish last half hour. And that would be only the first day. Which county could now do that regularly *from force of habit?*

Most of all, what Middlesex '47 gave to everyone willing to receive it was the joy of watching a noble spectacle and, without even knowing the pompous phrase, 'audience participation', joining in the fun. The enthusiasm of captain and team spread to spectators like a crackling prairie fire. People went to Lord's, just to see what Compton and Edrich were up to as their fathers had pursued the young Bradman and their great-grandfathers W. G. When Middlesex played Lancashire in their last match at Lord's, 60,000 people watched. It was virtually a thanksgiving service.

Last year on a sunless summer afternoon I observed Mr Sims, now the Middlesex scorer, listening with profound respect to a group of young players who were explaining to him how cricket was now a highly scientific game in which Compton and Edrich would look very small beer and in which progress had advanced so far that entertainment was impossible.

'True,' nodded Jim sagely, 'true. But there's just one thing. People used to come and watch us.'

I wish you could have seen his sublimely deadpan expression and I wish you would learn by heart *Wisden's* contemporary comment: 'Middlesex matches were attended by huge crowds. THEY SAW MATCH-WINNING CRICKET FROM TRUE CHAMPIONS!'

How long, O Lord's, how long . . .

Chapter Ten

NORTHAMPTONSHIRE, 1912

Northamptonshire have produced at least three elevens with high claims to be reckoned their brightest. Gaining first class status in 1905, they were the last county except Glamorgan to do so. They have not yet won the championship and, indeed, spent many seasons between the wars in the lowest depths, but they could never be guaranteed to be predictable, much less permanent, underdogs. In the last few seasons they have seldom strayed far from the top and in 1957 and in 1965 they were only pipped on the post by Surrey and then by Worcestershire.

Winning or losing, Northamptonshire have always worn a lighthearted air. Especially in earliest days, they would often play their cricket for fun, when concentration and hard grafting would have materially paid them better. They have not always enjoyed the sagest of captaincy, but when, as recently, inspiring leadership has been there, the lift has been high and unmistakable. They have not since the second war or, for that matter, since the first, relied to any great extent on local talent. I remember Brian Reynolds being first introduced to me as 'our one native', as though that excellent opening batsman were some kind of Man Friday. Of later captains, F. R. Brown came from Surrey, Dennis Brookes from Yorkshire and Keith Andrew from Lancashire. Probably the county's most colourful character was Valance Jupp, who emigrated from Sussex. There is something, however, about Northamptonshire, as there is in a perhaps even greater degree about Somerset, a mysterious spirit which takes a stranger, be he Australian, West Indian or even Yorkshireman, and stamps him as a loyal and permanent local man.

There was a minority of natives in the admirable eleven of 1965, who at the end of August had to sit, drumming their heels, while Worcestershire marched confidently, though at a very short distance, past them. This side I would set down as: (1) B. L. Reynolds, (2) C. Milburn, (3) R. M. Prideaux, (4) A. Lightfoot, (5) P. J. Watts, (6) D. S. Steele, (7) B. Crump, (8) M. E. Scott, (9) K. V. Andrew, captain, (10) H. Sully and (11) J. D. F. Larter. We could count as twelfth man P. D. Watts or M. E. Norman, both of whom have now moved with some success to other counties. Here was a tightly-knit team, with no outstanding batting stars, for Milburn had hardly yet launched himself into outer space as a hitter. They had, however, valuable all-rounders, as they still have, in P. J. (Jim) Watts, Steele and especially Crump, who came near to the double, and a varied selection of bowling from the slow stuff of Scott and Sully, through Crump, medium-fast, who took 112 wickets, to Larter, who was genuinely fast and seemed at the time the bowler England was looking for. A certain unlucky brittleness in health afterwards marred the fulfilment of these hopes, but no man can take five for 43 and seven for 37 against Yorkshire at Park Avenue without having had the root of the matter in him. Moreover, it was not only in Northamptonshire that Keith Andrew was reckoned England's most accomplished wicket-keeper.

The powerful team of 1957 had even more varied antecedents. Dennis Brookes, who came down from Yorkshire and qualified in the early 1930s, was, with Tom Dollery of Warwickshire, the most admirable of the early professional captains. The mere writing down of the names of this eleven, with their countries, counties or parishes, serves to show the global quality of their origins: (1) D. Brookes, Kippax (if anybody knows where that is), (2) P. Arnold, New Zealand, (3) L. Livingston, New South Wales, (4) D. W. Barrick, Fitzwilliam (where Geoff Boycott was born), (5) B. L. Reynolds,

Kettering, genuine native, (6) G. E. Tribe, Victoria, (7) J. S. Manning, South Australia, (8) F. H. Tyson, Bolton, Lancashire, (9) M. H. J. Allen, Bedford, (10) K. V. Andrew, Oldham, Lancs and H. R. A. Kelleher, born in Bermondsey and apprenticed in Surrey. In this near-foreign legion there was enormous strength. Five batsmen scored 1,000 runs, three bowlers took 100 wickets and these figures contained one of Tribe's half dozen doubles.

Powerful and sinewy as this eleven was, its achievements did not make so spectacular a leap forward as those of the team that reached the same championship position in 1912. This side was not so cosmopolitan, nor did it glitter with famous names; it is doubtful if it contained more than the odd name that has survived as a name, till now. They were, however, only in the eighth year of their first class existence, their previous positions out of 16 having been 13th, joint 11th, 15th, 15th, 7th, 9th (one below Yorkshire, whom they beat at Bramall Lane) and 10th. For most of this time they tended to be everybody's whipping-boy, though never so as did their successors between wars. There was one grisly game in 1907 in which they were dismissed by Gloucestershire for 12 runs, thus invoking the poignant telegram from headquarters: *Bring boys home at once Mother*. But 1912 was not 1907 and, as they leapt from tenth place to second, the old uncertainties and inhibitions were not so much stifled as chucked out, neck and crop. The reasons for their 1912 success were simple, but powerful. The chief reasons, moreover, were similar to those governing most cricketing successes: a battery of bowling, suitable to varied conditions, especially those of a wet summer; lively leadership; and the ability, generally shared with Yorkshire, to place the same eleven men in the field, match after match. In looking at so many of the less fashionable counties I have had to rummage about the 'also batted' to find a player worthy of nomination as twelfth man. With Northants 1912 the task was of the simplest. They only played twelve men. (In 1908 they had tried thirty-three.)

Man for man, they were not as individually gifted as, say, Kent, Lancashire or Middlesex, but they had the eager and skilled cohesion of a destroyer crew under a daring and popular skipper. This was the year of the triangular tournament and England played three Tests each against visiting Australians and South Africans, but such was the strength of the MCC side that had toured Australia the previous winter that few demands were made outside it. Consequently a team like Northamptonshire was able to pursue its purposeful way without any call-up for national service, though, to be just, England might have done worse than call up Sydney Gordon Smith or George Joseph Thompson.

This then was the team: (1) W. H. Denton, (2) W. East, (3) R. A. Haywood, (4) G. J. Thompson, (5) S. G. Smith, (6) J. S. Denton, (7) G. A. T. Vials, (8) John Seymour, (9) C N. Woolley, (10) W. Wells and (11) W. A. Buswell. Claude Woolley, right-handed brother of the illustrious Frank, acted as twelfth man during the first half of the season and 'Fanny' Walden, the tiny Tottenham winger, stood by for the second. As you might expect in a closely integrated unit, their batting was remarkable only in its consistency. Nobody managed an average of over 30 and only one, Buswell, their grizzled, farmerish-looking stumper, failed to average double figures.

There were four main bowlers, whose figures varied between S. G. Smith's devastating average of just over a dozen to East's just under 19. Smith, a tall, left-handed all-rounder from Trinidad, revelled in the pitches the wretched summer sent him and, though nobody scored 1,000 runs, his 827, added to his 100 wickets, brought him within striking distance of the double. On the season's play he could be counted as the side's foremost all-rounder. Coming over to England in 1906 with H. B. G. Austin's side, he headed their batting and bowling, taking especially heavy toll – twelve for 99 – from Northamptonshire. Asked to stay, he qualified as quickly as possible and instantly made his mark. Between 1909 and

1914 he did the double three times, performed three hat-tricks, hit one double-hundred and was the first Northamptonshire batsman to score 1,000 runs in a season. After the last pre-war season he was chosen as one of *Wisden's* Cricketers of the Year and after the war he went to New Zealand, playing cricket there till he was well into his fifties.

Thompson, by then aged 35, but looking older because of his luxuriant moustache, was almost a father figure symbolising his county's rise to first class status. The feeling that Northamptonhire could not long be left out of the first class reckoning, drew its strongest support from his progressive exploits as the most exciting all-rounder ever to stir the quiet backwater of the minor counties. A pupil of Wellingborough Grammar School, he was a big, burly fellow who played for his county at eighteen, bowled at a fast-medium pace with a horrid lift at the last split second, and batted like a man with a personal dislike of the ball. He had played in representative first class games before his county went up in the world and he was picked for England against Australia in 1909. In the match he scored 6, which was half a dozen more than Fry and Hobbs. The following winter he toured South Africa with P. F. Warner's side and was one of the successes of an unsuccessful rubber. He was the first minor counties bowler to take 100 wickets and in his ten first class seasons before the war, he took 100 wickets eight times. If his two doubles look skimpy against Jupp's ten, Tribe's six and S. G. Smith's three, remember that (a) Thompson *introduced* doubles into Northamptonshire and (b), apart from Broderick's single double in 1948, no other Northants man ever did the double at all. War wounds prevented Thompson from seriously picking up the threads of his career, but he did some valuable coaching. His career brought him 12,000 runs and just under 1,600 wickets and he could have been reckoned a tough model professional in any age.

From early days Bill East, also medium-fast, was his natural other-end support, a genial soul and a dependable opening bat.

Though seldom as penetrative a bowler as either Thompson or Smith, he had his days and would sometimes turn in an atomic individual performance, as when, going on at second change against Lancashire in 1911, he took seven for 11. William (Bumper) Wells earned his nickname with deliveries that came fast and flew high. He had served with the local regiment in the Boer war and bowled so destructively in Army games that peacetime found for him an almost automatic place in the county team. He batted, as he bowled, with heart and soul and, going in at No. 10, he thumped away contentedly. With a four-sided bowling instrument of this kind Northamptonshire had little need to call in anybody else.

Opening the innings with East was W. H. (Bill) Denton, whose twin brother, J. S. (Jack) generally batted at No. 6. Cricketing twins, such as the Rippons and Bedsers, have always posed problems of identification, but the Dentons were more indistinguishable than any of the others. Apart from being free-hitting batsmen with similar strokes, the burden they placed upon the scorers was almost crushing and this burden grew when, later, they became the county's opening pair. I feel that that delighful character, the county's present scorer would have worked out some ingenious system of recognition signals, but his predecessors remained worried men.

R. A. Haywood (No. 3) and John Seymour (usually No. 8), brother of the more celebrated Kent batsman, James Seymour, came in from outside to make their careers with Northamptonshire. Haywood was a tall, loose-limbed stylist who was a joy to watch when in full flight, while Seymour was a natural hitter who was also capable of breaking a stand as a change bowler. Until Milburn started hitting the ball into the neighbouring counties, he was the only man to lift one on to the roof of the Northampton Bowling Green pavilion. Like Albert Trott in similar circumstances, he was never quite the same man again.

This leaves us, apart from Walden and Woolley, who in 1912 played Cox and Box with the twelfth man position and were afterwards invaluable members of the eleven, with G. A. T. (Tubby) Vials, an ideal captain, quiet efficient, incapable of missing a trick for a team that was no firmament of glittering stars. He preferred to direct operations from No. 7 though later he was happy to go in first. He was a batsman discriminatingly capable of attack or defence at need, a shrewd tactician and one of the quickest outfield's in the competition. It was sad that, after three years' vigorous captaincy, the needs of his law practice took him back from crease to desk, but his interest has never cooled and for the last dozen years he has been his county's alert and honoured president.

Four members of this vintage eleven of 1912, including their captain, are alive today and it is fascinating to speculate how many of the runners-up in 1968 will be equally spry in 2024. Young readers might make a note to wonder about that.

Chapter Eleven

NOTTINGHAMSHIRE, 1929

Nottinghamshire's most shining achievement is that they have won the county championship a dozen times and shared it five times; their less impressive record is that they have not headed the table since 1929, and that their last successful season before that was in 1907. In the 1870s they disputed precedence practically alone with the Gloucestershire of 'the resistless Graces', while in the 1880s they found it hard, until Surrey began to grow in strength, to find a County worth disputing with. Sad to say, their almost unbroken run of victories ended in 1886; their next clear win came after a gap of twenty-one years and the next after that following a further gap of twenty-two. The two later elevens were fitting champions in their day and it should be a source of pride that two outstanding cricketers, W. R. D. Payton and George Gunn, covered the expanse of the years and were members of both.

One was an ideal professional cricketer, full of skill and character; the other was a wayward genius. It always worries me to use the word *genius,* with Sir Donald Bradman glancing sternly over one shoulder and W. G. glowering over the other, while the spirit of Sir Jack Hobbs, who never glowered, smiles in quizzical fashion. Nevertheless, if George Gunn was not a genius, then I am a Dutchman.

Taking the calculation over the seasons, I do not have to say which county, year in and year out, has had the most distinguished history. Your computer will tell you that. But an elderly Notts enthusiast might well say: 'Go easy, now. Before you were born we just kept the championship in the office, permanent-like, at Trent Bridge.' Nor would this be any idle boast, for in that period of sinewy strength, rarely would you see an England side without half a dozen men from Nottinghamshire: Flowers and William Barnes, lively all-rounders; William Gunn, tall classic batsman, and father-figure of the clan; Scotton, a stonewaller who would have made Trevor Bailey look like Colin Milburn; Shrewsbury, the dapper Test opener, neat in every movement as a new pin, whom W. G., after conscientious comparison, reckoned to be the second-best bat in England, and Mordecai Sherwin who, according to legend, began his career by walking in at the Trent Bridge main gate and announcing: 'I'm t'new county stumper!' A superb combination.

But all this happened long ago and far away and indeed the high pride of cricket in that age seems to carry a touch of fantasy. After so legendary a period there was a long gap and then the county came up again with a winning team, built, as winning sides are, on a pair of splendidly destructive bowlers, Hallam and Wass, on a foundation of solid but not inactive batting, and on the leadership of a fighting captain, A. O. Jones, who headed an MCC side in Australia and was the finest slip-field in the country in his day.

If I vote for the eleven of 1929, I admit there is not a great deal in it. The later side was not dissimilar in strength; was led with equal force and, besides some fairly rich batting talent, possessed, in Larwood and Voce, the most menacing pair of opening bowlers ever found in a county. It also con-tained – did I mention it? – the ineffable George Gunn. Here are the names of this eleven: (1) G. Gunn, (2) W. W. Whysall, (3) W. Walker, (4) W. R. D. Payton, (5) A. W. Carr, captain, (6) A. Staples, (7) B. Lilley, (8) F. Barratt, (9) H. Larwood, (10) W. Voce and (11) S. J. Staples. We often hear of a certain year being a batsman's year or a bowler's year and the weather is not without its effects and hazards, but where you have an outstanding team, both bats-men and bowlers compete to outshine each other and the result is success. In 1929 six men, Gunn, Walker, Payton, Carr, A. Staples and Whysall hit their 1,000, runs, Whysall's coming near to 3,000. Of the bowlers Barratt took 129 wickets, Voce 120, Larwood 117, A. Staples 82 and S. J. Staples 80. If they were not a team of all-rounders, they were undoubtedly an all-round team.

George Gunn's career lasted from 1902 to 1932, which was not bad for a man who never enjoyed perfect health. Without dispute, he was Nottinghamshire's most delightful batsman, playing according to his whim, strolling out to the fastest bowler and hitting him over his head, or defending with exasperating solidity, if speed were not of the essence. He often appeared to be answering some real or imaginary criticism by 'showing 'em' just how foolish the critics had been. He loved to choose his own tempo and stick to his own lunch-time. More perhaps than any other cricketer, he went his own way, not perversely, but with a beaming smile. Having lost part of the 1906 season with a lung-haemorrhage, he wintered in New Zealand and came back to take part in the triumphant season of 1907. The following winter he was sent by his friends to Australia to achieve full recovery from his lung troubles. With the MCC touring side suffering from illness and injuries, he was called in, hit two Test hundreds, and headed the tour's batting averages.

Altogether he hit more than 35,000 runs, including 62 centuries, and the charm of his batting was as youthfully refreshing at the end of his long career as at the beginning and it was characteristic that he should hit an elegant 164 not out on his fiftieth birthday. He even went to the West Indies in the winter that followed and with Sandham compiled an opening stand of 322 against Jamaica. No Notts' batsman scored more runs and no batsman of any county ever derived or dispensed more unexpected pleasure from his cricket.

His opening partner in their championship season was W. W. ('Dodge') Whysall, a prolific scorer whose life was cut short by an unhappy accident at the end of the following year. He enjoyed only ten years at the top, but scored 2,000 runs in five successive summers, reaching his high watermark in 1929, when his run-total was 2,716. His defence was immensely wary and in his forty first-wicket partnerships of over 100 with George Gunn he always looked the harder of the two to get out. Of his four England caps three were gained with A. E. R. Gilligan's 1924–25 tour and, in the most exciting match of the rubber, which England lost by only eleven runs, he was his side's highest scorer with 75, ravaged from the enemy in a valiant effort to save the game.

Nos. 3 and 4 were Walker and Payton, two natural games-players of the type that formed the backbone of county cricket and First League football elevens in pre-war days, steady, conscientious and ready to serve their sides without question. Walker, between 1913 and 1934, scored 18,242 runs for Notts and Payton, between 1905 and 1931, scored 22,132. Figures do not mean everything, but here they mean a lot. Walker was a League goal-keeper in the winter months and Payton was the father of another Notts' batsman, the Rev. W. G. E. Payton, of Cambridge University and the RAF, who also played the occasional game for Derbyshire.

Nottinghamshire have had many captains, from the solemn Alfred Shaw, more than half of whose overs in a long career were maidens, to the forceful ones, A. O. Jones, whose tenure of office included 1907, and A. W. Carr, who reigned in 1929. Everything about Arthur Carr was aggressive: his on-driving, his close-fielding and his fiery temperament, whose wrath even the soft answer of a George Gunn could not wholly turn away. (Not that that could perturb George.) Carr was England's unlucky captain in 1926, just as A. P. F. Chapman was the lucky one, but for Notts he was for sixteen years a dominating figure, especially in 1929, when his inspiration held his men to their highest pitch. A warm and generous friend, he could also be an over-eager partisan, whose counsel was not always of the wisest. But few Notts batsmen have hit more runs more attractively and no county has ever had a tougher fighter.

Apart from that expert wicket-keeper, Ben Lilley, who wore the gloves from 1921 into the 1930s, the rest of the side were bowlers, all first-class performers in their own right. Lilley was one of the imperturbable kind. He waited four years for a regular place behind the stumps until Tom Oates, the pre-war stumper retired. He survived comparison with his more celebrated namesake, Arthur Augustus (Dick) Lilley, who won 35 England caps, while Ben, like Dog Tray, got none. The fact is that when Ben was at his best (and among the best) Duckworth and Ames tended to monopolise the England gloves, though it was hotly argued at Trent Bridge that the man who could keep to Larwood and Voce could keep to anybody. He struck a Nottinghamshire record by being the first wicket-keeper to score 1,000 runs in a season and did it again three years later, just to show it was no flash in the pan. A friend of mine, playing for an unimportant county, went out to bat and to hear wicket-keeper and slip deep in conversation regarding the afternoon's racing. The first ball my friend received touched the edge of his bat. He saw the umpire's finger raised and, as he walked away, he heard Ben Lilley say, without any reference to the immediate matter in hand. 'I tell you, George, that horse has only got three legs.'

Winning teams, like the Yorkshire of the 1920s and the Surrey of the 1950s, are carried to success by their bowlers, whatever other virtues they may display. Yet I doubt if either Yorkshire or Surrey ever produced a battery more richly varied in its deadly fire-power – Larwood, Voce, Barratt and Arthur and Sam Staples, who in 1929 took 525 wickets between them. There will always be argument about the fastest of fast bowlers, from Richardson to Kortright; from Cotter to Gregory and McDonald; from Tyson to Trueman, but when it comes to comparison on calculated merit, on speed, perfection of control, beauty of action and the power to break through the strongest defence, Larwood in his greatest days stood supreme. In 1929 he had returned after a splendid tour with A. P. F. Chapman in Australia and county opponents reaped the whirlwind of his exuberant success. His second Australian tour was in the controversial 'body-line' tour of 1932–33, which brought much unhappiness to cricket. But unhappiness does not last for ever and he is now settled in Australia with his family, without a hint of ill feeling in sight.

The names of Larwood and Voce go naturally together. When both were bowling fast together, Larwood right-handed and Voce left, they could be as formidable a pair as Gregory and McDonald, but Voce could also bowl slow and so Notts, and England, had an extra string to their bows. His England caps were 27, half a dozen more than Larwood's, and his finest feats were accomplished with G. O. Allen's side in Australia in 1936–37.

The Staples brothers were foils both to their more distinguished colleagues and to each other. Sam bowled medium pace off an awkward-looking, shuffling run, and suffered the exasperation of being attacked by rheumatism just as he was running into form. Arthur, who was physically sturdier, was a much more accomplished bat and, besides taking 600 wickets for his county, hit over 2,000 runs.

The last of the 1929 quintuplets was F. Barratt, a fast bowler who batted just like one. After doing the double in 1928, he was honoured by a Test cap against South Africa in 1929, but took only two wickets. His method of speech was as sardonically robust as his figure was burly and there is an apocryphal account of a light-hearted tour match in which the umpire was continually 'calling' Fred for 'dragging'. Suddenly the batsman's middle stump went crashing and, as he walked away, the fielding captain walked up to the bowler's wicket.

'Fred,' he exclaimed in horror-stricken undertones, 'you *threw* that one.'

'I know, I know, skipper,' said Fred impenitently, 'but he was looking at my feet.'

W. G. Quaife, the staunch professional backbone of Warwickshire's
Champion team in 1911

WORCESTERSHIRE, 1964. *Above:* The 1964 team: *Back row (l. to r.):* W. Faithful (scorer), D. Slade, R. Headley, R. Carter, L. Coldwell, N. Gifford, C. Fearnley, W. Powell. *Front row:* R. Booth, J. Flavell, D. Kenyon (captain), T. Graveney, M. Horton, D. Richardson. *Below:* Style and hostility. Tom Graveney (*left*) and Len Coldwell both contributed greatly to the County's championship win

It may be thought that Notts supporters have looked on their county's present lowly status with complacency. On the other hand, they may be gazing forward into a happier future:

> *So tonight we'll merry, merry be,*
> *So tonight we'll merry, merry be,*
> *So tonight we'll merry, merry be,*
> *Tomorrow we'll have Sobers.*

Chapter Twelve

SOMERSET, 1966

Nothing is so predictable about Somerset as its complete unpredictability. Even the county club, founded over a hundred years ago, was born in another county. In a history at first-class level, officially begun in 1891, they have produced a galaxy of glittering names that artist for artist, could have put any other county in the shade. There is no blinking at the glitter. Granted a little adjustment from H. G. Wells's *Time Machine,* you could set down an eleven of such royal quality that it would induce in other vintage teams an unlikely touch of humility. Here is one: (1) L. C. H. Palairet, (2) J. C. W. MacBryan, (3) L. C. Braund, (4) H. Gimblett, (5) P. R. Johnson, (6) J. Martyn, (7) S. M. J. Woods whom we might as well appoint captain to save him the trouble of appointing himself; (8) M. F. Tremlett, (9) J. C. White, (10) A. W. Wellard and (11) E. F. Tyler. An old English magic that could harness the superb talents of these cricketers into one team on a given summer's day would be enchantment indeed.

This is the genuine oddity about Somerset and I cannot think of any county where so many of their most famous cricketers over the years were not to be found in the elevens of their most efficient season. Take the muster roll set down above, which ought to be sung to martial music, and this is by no means an exclusive one. It does not include John Daniell, who, always excepting the rip-roaring Sammy Woods, was Somerset's most celebrated captain. Daniell, known as the Prophet, though scarcely an Old Testament character, played his cricket like a Rugby international (seven caps). He was a leader of fine ferocity, who was once seen pushing a handcart bearing a cottage piano down the main street of Taunton. Asked the reason for this eccentric pilgrimage, he replied: 'I've just sold Somerset for an old song . . .'

But return to the head of my list. Half a century after he gave up playing, Lionel Palairet, dubbed like a mediaeval knight, is still batting's 'observed of all observers', the *beau ideal* of elegance and charm. Even among his peers of the golden age, artists of the quality of R. E. Foster and R. H. Spooner, he was, and remains to this day, the true portrait of the artist as a young man. Yet never during his most fascinating days did Somerset come higher than eighth in the table. Master of all the elegances, he set the tradition of true grace, as followed by P. R. Johnson and J. C. W. MacBryan, both artists to their batting-glove tips.

Without doubt Somerset's greatest all-rounder, Leonard Braund, who qualified by way of W. G.'s London County at the turn of the century and, winning 23 caps, 20 of them against Australia, was seldom absent from an England side at the time of England's greatest power. Even Uncle Walter agreed that (a) Braund as an all-rounder was worthy to be named in the same proud ranks of the greatest as Hirst, Rhodes and F. S. Jackson, and that (b), as a slip-field, even the long-armed Tunnicliffe was not his master. This was harsh doctrine, but I had to accept the voice of authority. I would not more have resisted Uncle Walter's Laws of the Medes and Persians than Joan of Arc would have resisted her Voices.

Nor was this all. In Harold Gimblett, the young farmer from Watchett, Somerset produced in the 1930s the most consistent fast-scoring batsman who had appeared for many a long day. Here was a man who hit because apparently he enjoyed hitting, and the fact that he played for England three times only marks the agony of doubt that swift scoring so often seems to rouse in the melancholy breasts of selectors. As a batsman, he was the completely uninhibited citizen. Poor health shortened his career, but most batsmen would have envied his 50 centuries, his sparkling debut of 123 in 1935 and his as yet unchallenged highest of 310 for Somerset.

Arthur Wellard, a lively fast bowler, was not so much a quick scorer as an economic one. If he could gently acquire five sixes in an over, which he did on more than one occasion, he felt he had a happy knack of conserving his energies. Of the 11,000 runs acquired in his career, well over a third were accumulated in sixes. There is a legend of Wellard and the powerful amateur, G. F. Earle, leaning back at Taunton and placidly placing ball after ball in the river, while between overs Arthur Wood, the old Yorkshire wicket-keeper, goes stumping to the other end, darkly muttering: 'Look at them two, putting on sixes, *playing defensive . . .*'

John Cornish White was Somerset's captain between 1927 and 1931, and his feats of endurance with A. P. F. Chapman's team in Australia in 1928/9 stamped him as England's most ingenious slow bowler between Wilfred Rhodes and Hedley Verity. As for Sammy Woods, an Australian who played for England against South Africa and for Australia against England, he was literally larger than life and twice as exuberant. Batting, bowling, fielding and talking, he lived his life at full gallop. When in 1901 Somerset beat Yorkshire at Headingley by 273 runs, he leaped into a hansom cab and, normally the most loquacious of mortals, never gave utterance until he collapsed against the bar of the Queen's Hotel and emitted the beautiful word: 'Cham . . . pagne.'

The great, good and happy men of Somerset lacked nothing but one virtue – collective efficiency. Brilliant and delightful as individuals, they were, except for Braund, and Tyler who once took all ten Surrey wickets in an innings of 49, almost all gifted amateurs who played when they were free. Sammy Woods laid an unerring finger on the spot. 'There's Lord Hawke,' said Sammy. 'On the first of May he'll get a bit of pencil and write down twelve names on a bit of paper. By July those twelve names are still there, while I'll have written down fifty.' So much for gaiety, so much for fun and, right up to the Second World War, Somerset savoured her fun, probably more richly than any body of cricketers has ever done. As described by R. C. Robertson-Glasgow, the beloved Crusoe, hilarious entertainment and pretty good cricket cannot have been more delightfully blended.

Post-war cricket came in with a cold utilitarian wind, though the gleaming summer of 1947 saw Somerset, mainly through the all-round resources of an attractive youngster named Tremlett, tumble the champions. However erratic they might be, they were always good for a giant-killing or two. The 1950s were hardly a flourishing period for anybody except Surrey, but, in lighter or darker days, Somerset, that small sparsely-populated county, followed the bent that had always made them so attractive. They took in players from all over the world; but, Australian or West Indian or even Lancashireman, whatever you were, by the time you had served a season, you were Somerset, born and bred, and would never have lived anywhere else. There was a touch of this in the earliest days and, as time went on, there was more than a touch.

In 1958 the side included two Australians, a West Indian and cricketers from more than one northern English county. This was an eleven of bristling efficiency and reached a higher rung on the ladder than ever before.

Eight seasons later Somerset again reached a similar position, but one that was far more firmly based. Out of 28 county matches, they won 13, a more satisfactory total than ever before. They were cosmopolitan, and good luck to them, but in no era has a Somerset eleven shown tighter cohesion than in 1966. They were: (1) R. Virgin, a Taunton man, (2) G. G. Atkinson, a Yorkshireman from Lofthouse, (3) M. Kitchen, from Nailsea, home of beautiful glassware, (4) W. E. Alley, from Sydney, (5) A. Burgess, from romantic Glastonbury, (6) C. R. M. Atkinson, captain, from northeast Yorkshire, (7) K. E. Palmer, from Hampshire, (8) G. Clayton, Lancashire, (9) P. J. Robinson, nephew of the celebrated Roly Jenkins of Worcestershire, from Worcestershire, (10) B. Langford, from Birmingham, and (11) Fred Rumsey, a true Londoner, of those, perhaps three could be called true natives; the rest were Somerset by adoptive absorption.

A glance at their day-to-day figures underlines their practical value: no batsman averaged 30, but five of them scored their thousand runs; three bowlers took their hundred wickets each, and with two colleagues more, captured nearly 450 wickets between them. Ken Palmer's double was his first, without prejudice to further doubles, and fitted in nicely with the side's policy of direct attack.

Virgin and Graham Atkinson produced no such first-wicket spectacular of 362 as did Palairet and H. T. Hewett in 1892, but some 70 seasons later, they piled up 208 against Hampshire at Dean Park and in a quiet way right through the summer they gave their side a number of quiet, sturdy starts. Kitchen, a slow starter at No. 3, gradually consolidated his position and his fine physical strength, and led the side's batting, with every prospect, at the age of 26, of going further and faring better still.

At No. 4 Somerset had, at the seemingly impossible age of 47, the justly renowned, William E. Alley. He was, according to *Wisden,* born in Sydney in 1919, and, since I believe everything I read, especially in *Wisden,* I have no hesitation in regarding Bill Alley as an ageless, tireless character, if not a wholly fictional one; in 1961, a season of personal triumph, he joined the small post-war band of batsmen – Compton, Hutton, Edrich and Mike Smith – who had scored 3,000 runs in a season, and had gone on forming the county's backbone, with bat, ball and personality. He became, indeed, the perfect example of the stranger who has been so happily taken in. Beginning English county cricket at an age when most players take their benefits and retire, he has now been for ten years Somerset's most typical duck farmer and could be exhibited anywhere as such. It was hard to see any end to this delightful state of affairs, for Alley continued to have runs and wickets under his belt and, wherever duck eggs appear, ducklings will be hatched. Burgess, a big strong fellow well-known in local football, gradually forced his way into the batting order at No. 5.

Colin Atkinson was in his second year of captaincy and was continuing to contribute more than some stubborn batting and some useful leg-break bowling. By then he had developed a genuine flair for leadership which was part of the drive that helped to bring the county their well-lined bag of victories and only Yorkshire, the champions, and Worcestershire, the runners-up, were able to seize more. You do not advance so brightly without tact, wisdom and some penetrative cricket dispensed from the top. Atkinson is a member of the staff at Millfield, whose headmaster, R. J. O. Meyer, was Somerset's captain in 1947 and has built up a reputation for a kind of genius in picking academic brains and athletic skills. He will enigmatically admit to being 'a bit of a Robin Hood', because, by charging wealthy parents heavy fees, he has been able to give a wider education to some talented boys and girls who would not otherwise have so happily benefited.

To see Ken Palmer bowling in full flight is a joy to the critic and a qualm of disturbance to the batsman; between his debut in 1955 and the end of the county's best season he had scored over 6,000 runs and taken 744 wickets. His speed is below authentically fast, but his zip off the pitch, especially in his first few overs is completely disconcerting. He has taken 100 wickets four times and earned an England cap on the 1964–65 tour of South Africa. A most interesting link in the team's bowling chain was P. J. Robinson, a cunning left-hand slow bowler, who has since continued to exploit his gifts, and is a snapper-up of unconsidered trifles in the slips. In 1953 Brian Langford, a tall off-break bowler, had a startling beginning, taking 14 Kent wickets in his second match and, afterwards, put up some devastating sorties, including a nine for 26 against Lancashire in 1958. In this summer of 1966, he came back in a blaze to take his 112 wickets.

From the days of H. Martyn, M. D. Lyon and H. W. Stephenson, Somerset have never lacked wicket-keepers. When Lancashire in 1964 had one of their euphemistically named 'shake-ups', Clayton joined Somerset by special registration and his success in both conduct and accomplishment was not to be challenged.

Fred Rumsey, at No. 11, made an ideal whipper-in to this country eleven. He is big, heavy, even shambling in his longish run-up and on a wicket that endears itself to him, as I have seen more than once at Bath, the fur begins to fly and a wicket-keeper of Clayton's quality is heaven's gift to his side. Rumsey's England caps totalled five: one against Australia, one against South Africa, and three against a toughly resistent New Zealand. The way of a big, heavy, fast left-hander is never easy.

But the sheer professionalism of that side ... There were no loose ends or chinks in the armour. If you have a captain who knows his business as well as Colin Atkinson, all you need is a core of five bowlers, who averaged 88 wickets between them in this remarkable season, and eleven fielders, in the pink of condition, all on their toes. There is no reason to doubt that Somerset '66 represents their brightest season so far. True, they came third; in some other season with such records, they might have come first.

Chapter Thirteen

SURREY, 1955

It is a pleasant but quite disingenuous fancy of mine that if teams of outstanding skill and merit have shone brightly in periods (a) near to the present day and (b) back in the days which seem old-fashioned to those who are now young, the more recent story may well appear to be the vintage one. This could not be a cast-iron principle, but what do you feel about the history of Surrey?

Most people remember, and most people have seen at some time or another, the Surrey teams that between 1952 and 1958 carried off an unbroken succession of championships, seven in a row, with a kind of professional arrogance never, or hardly ever, seen before.

Surrey have not had an outright success since 1958, but the glow and gleam of victory remain. But their success was not a nine-days' wonder; it was without doubt a wonder, but a seven-seasons' wonder. Can you imagine a side playing seven seasons of 24 hard county games each: that is, 168 matches on the trot and out of that total winning 121. I cannot find any county that ever achieved that. The royal progress went forward under two leaders: for five years under Stuart Surridge, who, in determination, is often compared to Brian Sellers, whom I think of as an equally strong but rather less subtle character; and two under Peter May, who in his all too short day was the greatest batsman in the world, the greatest *young* batsman, merely because he retired too early. With such a story to tell, can any other tale compete with it? The extraordinary answer is in the affirmative.

The straightforward championship figures show Yorkshire to have won 30 times and Surrey 17, but the fact is that from the decent regularisation of the competition in 1873 into a form we understand, Yorkshire did not come up champions for 20 years, while Surrey took the pennant five times and shared it once. It was in the late 1880s and the early 1890s that they suddenly burst into brilliance and it is arguable – who can say the last word? – that the side led by J. K. Shuter or K. F. Key was as powerful and attractive as any sides seen since. I do not know if there are any old gentlemen still alive who, as boys, saw any of these lordly elevens; boys brought up in Surrey's true traditional loyalties by fathers and uncles who divided their time between their families and the Oval. If such remain even in a third generation, I am sure they will secretly roll round their tongues such names as Maurice Read, Walter Read, Tom Richardson, Bill Lockwood and those two superb all-rounders, Bill Brockwell and the delicate George Lohmann. These were, for two generations at least, names to conjure with. Lockwood, who had both his moments and his matches, and whose two deadly spells of bowling in 'poor Tate's match' might easily have changed its name to 'Lockwood's match.' As for Richardson, he was an indomitable character who captured over 1,000 wickets in four seasons and in a famous Test bowled and bowled and bowled until he dropped. And yet . . . Praisers of the old elevens are brave enough to praise what they never saw and one of the puzzles we shall never solve is: how would batsmen of the quality of Abel or Brockwell deal with the cunning of Lock or Laker or, if it comes to that, would the terrific speed of Richardson have disturbed the gifted calm of May? However imaginary the battle, it would not have been a sham fight.

There are those who will account it blasphemy not to put first, without argument, Surrey's victory of 1914, incidentally their last for nearly 40 years. A blasphemy, too, to pick any team which did not include Hobbs, P. G. H. Fender, Bill Hitch and Tom Rushby. But they have their places in Valhalla, even if Hobbs smiles whimsically at the thought.

So we return, only half repentant, through the mists to nearer our time. 'Modern cricket' has had the rough edge of the old 'uns tongues and has, owing to a series of misunderstandings, been called dull, unimaginative and unromantic. There may be something in this, but not much. Indeed, cricket being the wonderfully rich and resilient game it is, just as it is being denounced as tedious, it breaks out into a lambent flame in MCC's last tour of the West Indies, which is surely more romantic and more accumulatively breath-taking than anything since the beginning of Tests. Romantic matches, yes: the staggering tied game at Brisbane in 1960–61, which still leaves a credibility gap; or the Lord's match in 1963 when Cowdrey came out on a murky evening, his broken arm strapped to his side and the prospect of ten minutes on the rack before him. But neither of these pulsing dramas had touched the heart of cricket *in excelsis* like the last over of the last Test at Georgetown, Guyana, while Jeff Jones fought blindly for his life against the most diabolical bowling in the world and menacing fieldsmen with arms six feet long eager to pick his pocket.

If this romantic comedy of the 1960s seems some distance from the Surrey of the 1950s, this is illusory. It was Surridge's practical, businesslike lines of sheer professionalism that carried Surrey forward. Even in the days of amateur captains the most 'professional' county captains were Yorkshire's Sellers of the 1930s and Surrey's Surridge of the 1950s. In the romantic Caribbean rubber of 1967–68 was one of Surridge's talented youngsters and he has remained to do Surrey and England high credit.

To call either Sellers or Surridge a strong character would have been a breathless understatement. I once heard Sellers say: 'If we can't get first, second's as bad as bottom,' and he would give to the word *bottom* the most degraded intonation he could imagine. Both men came from successful business and cricketing families. Both had been trained in

the practical. But in no sense was Surridge a carbon copy of
the older man. Both were strong characters; both went their
different ways, but Surridge's simplicity led to a kind of stream-
lining. You didn't mind if the other skipper won the toss.
Let him get in and lose a wicket or two and see how he liked
it. Let the enemy be subject to the toughest bowling of the
time and the uncanniest pick-pocketing fielding of *any* time
and wonder what was happening to him.

Granted the flowing merits of a seven-year ceaseless tide,
how does one pick out a season? It cannot be that it was the
same eleven all through, though, if you flip through your
Wisdens, you will find honest folk who apparently wanted
to be in on everything. When the run began one or two
old men-at-arms were on the point of retiring and, when it
ended, a number of the faithful were wearing well. Their
second championship saw them being driven at increasing speed
along the path that Surridge had ordained. To call such progress mechanical is not belittling; the noble Rolls Royce engine
is just a bit of machinery.

Not many championship sides come through the conflict
with 20 or more wins to their credit: 20 in 1952, 23 in
1955 and 21 in 1957 were Surrey's tally. An even more
astonishing thing is that in 1955 there was not a drawn
game in the whole season. Five matches were lost, but obviously
in an effort to snatch quick runs. Strategy and tactics were
faultless and driving towards the goal had a touch of the
Juggernaut about it.

Therefore, I would choose 1955, season of a South African
visit, which involved calls on at least three Surrey players.
The eleven was: (1) M. J. Stewart, (2) T. H. Clark, (3) P.
B. H. May, (4) K. F. Barrington, (5) B. Constable, (6) A. J.
McIntyre, (7) J. C. Laker, (8) P. J. Loader, (9) G. A. R.
Lock, (10) W. S. Surridge, (11) A. V. Bedser. Moreover,
it would be unjust not to mention that Surrey could call upon
batsmen of the style and calibre of David Fletcher, whom
only flawed health kept from the highest honours, and Eric

Bedser, an all-rounder so versatile he could puzzle himself.

What can you say of a team of eleven characters, all of whom are world figures in their own right? What of Alec Bedser, around whom England built successful Test teams and who produced fantastic bowling figures until time, Trueman and Statham sailed past them? What could you say of Peter May, who, from his school days, scored 85 centuries and made only one false stroke in his life? I may be wrong, but my very private opinion is that it broke his heart. Or what of Lock and Laker, whose tricks and resources should have been set down by a psychiatrist and no mere reporter. In the far Australian bush there are still anguished mothers who calm their recalcitrant offspring: 'Belt up, you little perishers, or I'll fetch Jim Laker to you . . .' When in 1956 Laker at the Oval took ten wickets in the Australian first innings, and then in the Old Trafford Test he 'impossibly' took 19 wickets for 90, you were not obliged to believe it. It is a matter of credibility; sometimes I don't believe it myself. As for Tony Lock, I always seem to see him as a leaping figure; leaping to take 'impossible' catches in the leg-trap; leaping back to take Leicestershire to the highest point in their history; leaping back for winter recreation to win the Sheffield Shield for his state; and then, after little more than a bath and change, leaping anti-clockwise back into the Caribbean to do the West Indies a bit of no good.

Bernard Constable was one of cricket's oddities. Until an accident to his knee, he was the fleetest of fielders. Nobody could call him a great batsman, but he was as hard to dislodge as a granite boulder. I have spent the evening with north-country bowlers, ruefully recalling a hard day in the field: 'If hadn't been for that so-and-so Bernie, life at Bramall Lane would have been one grand sweet song . . .' Had he not been so well-loved a character I tremble to think what might have happened to him.

It has always been my private view that Arthur McIntyre was the finest, least obtrusive wicket-keeper of his time. When we meet I shake my head in solemn reproach. He knows what I mean: *You retired too soon.* This is impertinence on my part because he only retired from behind the stumps to become the county's chief coach. And what an excellent bat he was: bold, aggressive, never willing to accept a defensive position. Few batsmen have taken gayer pleasure in dealing with a deadly attack like a bomb disposal unit.

So it comes, not only to having the best batsman in the world, but a lesser batting array that would get on with the job quickly enough to let the bowlers do their destructive duty. It also comes, of course, to having the most varied attack seen in the counties for years. Imagine yourself wilting under the sheer ferocity of Peter Loader or the bewildering skills of Alec Bedser and fleeing to the other end to the wheedling invitations of Laker or Lock. Imagine the impossible: avoiding the close-fielding of Stewart, who took 52 catches that summer and was to take many more, Barrington, the incredible Lock and Surridge.

Surridge in many ways was more incredible still. His bulk was menacing, like the ideal rugger forward's, yet he would dive to a low catch with all the agility of Stewart, the youngest member of the inner ring. Though a batsman with a keen eye, good for a quick 50 most days, he would seldom put himself in higher than No. 8. He was equally modest in bowling, taking his turn late, but never finishing the season without a reasonable bag.

And naturally there was leadership. Surridge, like Sellers, had an elemental force in his composition, but leadership has something which is not allied to brute force. Stuart Surridge had this in abundance. Nobody has had it in the same degree since.

Chapter Fourteen

SUSSEX, 1932

There is an ancient fairy tale in which gifts are richly bestowed on the favoured infant at its christening, but, owing to some secretarial error, Fairy Nettlesting is not invited, and she secretly inserts a sting in the tail of all its gifts. Sussex have had periods of this mysterious frustration. At the turn of the century, and especially in 1902 and 1903, when they ran second in the table, they possessed in Ranjitsinhji and C. B. Fry the two most brilliant batsmen in England and, with the possible exception of Victor Trumper, the most brilliant in the world. But during the same period their attack was ordinary; not negligible, of course, for it was borne by the excellent Fred Tate who in 1902, his fatal year, took 153 wickets; George Cox senior, who lived to go out in a blaze of glory twenty-two years later (fifteen for 106 at the age of 53) and Albert Relf, the county's most accomplished all-rounder except the incomparable Maurice Tate. Such an attack allied to a mediocre batting side might have appeared formidable, but C. B. Fry and Ranjitsinhji were there to prove that if this was golden age of batting, it was difficult for it to be the golden age of bowling, too.

Sixty years later, when Sussex undoubtedly possessed in E. R. Dexter the most dazzling batsman of a short but genuinely brilliant period, I have watched Ian, my indefatigable namesake, pounding away cheerfully, over after over, summer after summer, never missing his hundred wickets in a dozen seasons and capable of getting them in his sleep. The pitches at Hove, particularly on sun-drenched Saturdays, were enough to break any heart less stout than Ian Thomson's. I once saw him take all ten wickets in a single innings but this was at Worthing and he finished on the losing side.

Never the time and the place, then, and the loved one all together? Happily, not so. The time came in the late 1920s and early 1930s. Here was Maurice Tate, as unchallenged in his sphere as Ranjitsinhji and Fry had been in theirs. What was just as vital was that a Prince Charming walked in and, with a smile, swept away the spell of the wicked fairy. The prince was a true prince, Kumar Shri Duleepsinhji, a person of rare charm and a batsman of exquisite artistry. The summer when Tate and A. E. R. Gilligan, bowling for England, got rid of South Africa for 24 marked a high peak in English bowling success, but an unhappy accident to Gilligan cut short the bite and edge of his speed, so that never again were Sussex able to mount so devastating a two-pronged attack. But Tate went on from strength to strength in an almost unending series of finest hours.

Duleepsinhji had a 'good boy's' career at Cheltenham and, though physically frail, was a tower of strength on going up to Cambridge. He played for eight seasons only, but scored 15,537 runs, including 50 centuries, and took 243 catches, mostly at slip and generally at terrific speed. Joining Sussex, his uncle's old county, he played from 1926 till 1932, missing 1927 because of severe illness. He gave freely to the game what we have no right to demand of any cricketer. His play, in its elegance, grace and power, was the perfect expression of his radiant personality, naturally friendly, humorous and gay and always engaged in a struggle, outwardly visible to nobody, with imperfect health.

I would call the side captained by Duleepsinhji in 1932 the most gifted eleven, even though they still came only second. It is impossible to exaggerate the happy influence he exercised on Sussex during a career which now seems even shorter than it really was.

In 1928 they were sixth in the table and Duleep headed the county averages with 60.

Yorkshire dominated the Championship in the three years prior to the last war, with Herbert Sutcliffe (*left*) and Bill Bowes just two of an outstanding team of cricketers. *Below:* A picture to relish! Yorkshire batting against Kent at Tonbridge in the '30s, with Leyland hitting out, Ames keeping wicket and Woolley in the slips

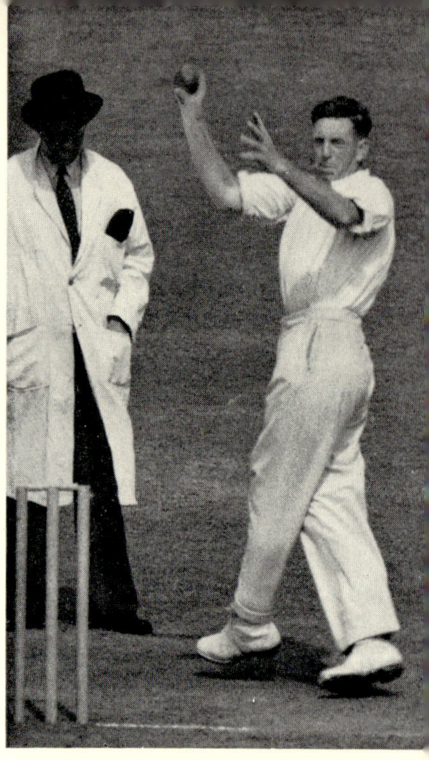

Bowlers win matches, so it is said, and these four certainly contributed much to their Counties' successes! *Above:* Bill Copson (Derbyshire) and *(left)* Yorkshire's Hedley Verity. *Below:* J. C. Clay of Glamorgan *(left)* and Middlesex's own Jim Sims

In 1929 they improved their position by one, the match of the season being a terrific game with Kent in which Duleep scored 115 and in the second innings an incredibly dashing 246. All this, with five more hundreds and a county average of 56 were his practical contribution.

In 1930 it was a summer to send chroniclers and even scorers reeling back. Playing for England against Australia Duleep scored a glittering 173 and against Northamptonshire at Hove he hit 333, which remains the highest score by a Sussex batsman, even higher than his uncle's previous record of 283 not out. The innings was a superb tour de force. It took five and a half hours and must have been the swiftest effort of sustained batsmanship ever made by an artist of frail physique. There was a close, almost psychic relationship between uncle and nephew. As the uncle grew older, he became more and more of a perfectionist, while the nephew never modified his attitude of respect, even reverence. When at the end of his glorious Test innings against Australia he was caught off a huge ballooning hit in the deep, Ranji said: 'The boy just can't concentrate . . .' It would have been difficult to criticise the magnificent 333, but there were of course some failures and near failures which bore in their train shoals of gibing telegrams, one of which ran: *Go and play tennis with Betty Nuttall.*

'That,' said Duleep imperturbably, 'is one of the milder ones.'

Nothing could happen that would break the golden link between them.

In 1931 Duleep was appointed county captain and Sussex took another leap forward. They finished fourth in the table and Duleep was not far off 2,000 runs in the county aggregate, with an average of 58. Tate took his customary, almost statutory, 100 wickets, while young A. F. (Bert) Wensley had a handsome bowling season. And now we come to 1932, the year of destiny.

As it had been for several seasons, the eleven was wonderfully compact, but with Duleepsinhji and Tate answering the call of their country, there were capable reserves standing by. In his second season of leadership Duleep continued his welding of eleven highly gifted cricketers into a flexible machine almost impossible to stop. When I look at the scorecard I am dazed by the sheer fire-power of the players. Here are the names on paper: (1) E. H. Bowley, (2) J. H. Parks, (3) K. S. Duleepsinhji, captain, (4) T. E. Cook, (5) John Langridge, (6) James Langridge, (7) H. W. Parks, (8) R. S. G. Scott, (9) A. F. Wensley, (10) M. Tate, (11) W. Cornford. This team came second and, in point of fact, an ebullient Sussex also came second the following season and, for full measure, the season after that.

But I could never be shaken in my faith in 1932. It was Duleep's swan-song and I would not choose a season which passed him by. I have said that in that season I found the sheer weight of these cricketers' achievements crushing. In the table of averages there are three batsmen who scored well over 1,000 runs in the county season: Duleepsinhji, 1094 in all matches, Bowley, and H. W. Parks; three more, James Langridge (1192 in all matches), J. H. Parks (1105 in all matches) and T. E. Cook were hardly, in county games, a whisker away. Tate was England's outstanding bowler, the most devastating between S. F. Barnes and Alec Bedser. His season's bag was 124 (in all matches 160). He had not, of course, as he sometimes humorously complained, been bowling at both ends. He had had an invaluable partner in James Langridge who took 92 county wickets (in all matches 115) and A. F. Wensley 81 (in all matches 104). A lesser but valuable help came from R. S. G. Scott, a talented Oxford Blue who had fought the good fight in the University match. He played only two seasons for Sussex, of which this was the first and the better. He took only 54 wickets but every one, you might say, was a coconut. Wensley was a young bowler, rising twenty, coming along determined to go somewhere, anywhere . . .

The wicket-keeper over this rising period was a tiny one, and, against so vast a surface as the Hove ground, virtually invisible to the naked eye. His name was Walter Cornford, and his size was considerably smaller than that of anyone now playing, except Henry Pilling of Lancashire. If you were so foolish as to believe that this little man behind you was not paying strict attention to business, wisdom was not with you. He was a man who could deal with the contrastingly subtle variations of pace of Tate, James Langridge, Bert Wensley. You might make an error of judgment in any fraction of these matters, *he* never would. They called him Tich on account of his size, but this was not satire, even gentle satire. It was a compliment to one who was part of their friendly landscape. Wicket-keepers do not as a rule have a massive batting average, though Cornford's was more than adequate. Their records are counted in victims like an Indian's scalps. His trophies were not as numerous as those of the Terror of the Palefaces, Herbert Strudwick, whose victims reached the grisly total of 1493, but, playing through the period between wars, Tich accumulated a nice little heap of foolish victims, 639 caught and 314 stumped. His proudest achievement was to have twice stumped Hobbs on the leg-side in one match.

The batting of the side was so strong both in attack and defence that I can only contemplate it once more with awe. E. H. (Ted) Bowley was one of the most prolific scorers of his time, a No. 1 to give confidence to any side, weak or strong. A genial, kindly soul, it was natural that, when he retired, he was invited to be coach at Winchester, the plum of all school coaching jobs. In his last season he hit 283, the highest score ever compiled by a Sussex professional, and rode cheerfully out on a storm of praise and affection. His excellent bowling record, not to mention his prehensile fielding, would have gained him a place in memory. In mid-career were the brothers Parks; Harry, a persistently heavy scorer, and Jim, father of *our* Jim, the only man to make 3,000 runs and take 100 wickets in one season, while thrusting past him were the run-greedy Langridges, John and James, the only Sussex batsmen among those who have scored 30,000 (all matches). James was almost as efficient a run-maker as his brother and as keen a wicket-snatcher as Tate. John, now a Test umpire, took more slip-catches, including 69 in 1955, than anybody between Hammond and Philip Sharpe. A long-limbed picker-up of un-considered trifles of the build of Tunnicliffe, his last season's bag was his best.

I do not normally bow down before figures, but no personal praise can outweigh the statistics of this county eleven from start to finish of their careers:

		Runs for county	Wickets for county
1.	E. H. Bowley	25,439	670
2.	J. H. Parks	19,720	795
3.	K. S. Duleepsinhji	9,180	5
4.	T. E. Cook	20,176	80
5.	John Langridge	34,152	44
6.	James Langridge	28,884	1,416
7.	R. S. G. Scott	1,478	90
8.	H. W. Parks	21,673	13
9.	A. F. (Bert) Wensley	7,995	1,054
10.	M. W. Tate	17,086	2,211
11.	W. Cornford	6,327	—

With no bowler of the calibre of Tate, who earned 39 England caps, the burdens at the other end were bravely borne that season by Wensley and James Langridge. The years went on, players grew older and were lost to sight, but their colossal batting figures remain hugely mountainous and I will save the purchase of a comptometer by saying that the runs made for Sussex by that eleven in their separate careers added up to 192,110.

By mid-August Sussex were riding high and their firm grip on the second place was deservedly popular, with the possible exception of hard-hearted men between Barnsley and Bradford, with every cricketer in the kingdom. They had the greatest bowler of the age, Maurice Tate, who, though a seasoned veteran of 37, remained astonishingly at the height of his powers; they also had the most popular captain. Tate's bag for Sussex was colossal; his lifetime's accumulation of 2,783, 155 of them in Tests, was worthy of display on any man's tombstone.

Then things began to happen like the climax of a Greek tragedy or, more closely, like the trials of Job. Duleep had been unable to play in the earlier August matches but on the 24th, day of the fateful return Yorkshire match, always a peak of the year, it became known that his old illness had struck him down, and, even more depressing, that he would not play again that season, that he might never play again. This was the cruellest blow, but not the only one, for Bowley, their most cheerfully reliable bat, and Wensley, Tate's most dependable bowling partner, were seriously injured. The side was still strong and the reserves brought in had creditable careers: A. Melville, the Oxford captain, J. Cornford, an excellent medium-pace bowler and George Cox, well-loved by a later generation. But Yorkshire had their teeth in the red meat. They started with a grim struggle against Tate's heroic six for 79, but Sussex, except for Cook, crumpled before Bowes (eight for 62); then Sutcliffe hit an immaculate hundred, his sixth in a dozen consecutive innings, and Bowes and Verity coaxed the Sussex innings to curl up and die. They had one more match in which to retrieve a point or two, but when victory seemed possible, fate again turned cruel. In the last over eight runs were needed with two wickets to fall; the careful John Langridge was run out and the game closed down, a mildly inglorious end to a season of glory.

Chapter Fifteen

WARWICKSHIRE, 1911

BY DENZIL BATCHELOR

Lord Randolph Churchill in an immortal phrase declared that 'great men make mistakes. Napoleon forgot Blücher. I forgot Goschen.' The world of cricket has often been guilty of forgetting Warwickshire, which is just as bad as either of the other major lapses. It forgot the county in 1911, and again in 1951: and on both occasions it won the Championship. And then it surprised humanity by winning the Gillette Cup of 1966. There was a certain amount of excuse for forgetting Warwickshire in 1911. In that year they had a 22-year-old untested captain, F. R. Foster, and were one but bottom of the table half-way through the season: and they won the championship when all depended on the last game. In 1951 they were the first county to win the championship with a professional captain, H. E. 'Tom' Dollery, and a professional team. They played one amateur only, and he only played once.

Let us consider the earlier side first. Foster was a cricketing genius. He was a left-handed bowler above medium pace, with a superb swerve even in Adelaide's limpid atmosphere: the ball straightened up just before it reached the bat. He had a slow ball too, hard to spot.

You always hear of Barnes and Foster in Australia in 1911/12. That is because Barnes took those five wickets for six runs at Melbourne on the morning of December 30th. It was no wonder that Hitch, crossing over after four had gone, muttered to Hobbs: 'Jack, we've won the match.'

Warwickshire, 1911 – by Denzil Batchelor

Don't forget when you say Barnes and Foster, that Barnes played for Warwickshire in his time and might have played for them up till the First World War, had pay and conditions been right. Barnes and Foster indeed, but when the tour was over Frank Foster was top of the bowling averages in the Tests, as well as in *all* matches. An injury in a motor-cycle accident finished his cricketing career at twenty-five. He was a superb hard-hitting batsman as well as a bowler-and-a-half. He once made 305 not out against Worcestershire, helping 'Tiger' Smith add 166 in 70 minutes.

But his greatest day of all was Friday, January 12th, 1911, when on a plum wicket he switched his three slips to close on-side fields and clean bowled Kelleway and Armstrong, got Hill dazzlingly stumped on the leg side, lured Hordern to offer a catch to Rhodes, and bowled Minnett. He didn't get Armstrong who made 33 of Australia's 133 because he slipped and fell when running in to catch and bowl him: but he did, in that spell, take five wickets for nineteen runs in nineteen overs.

But of course it was the Warwickshire team that triumphed in 1911: C. S. Baker, C. Charlesworth, F. E. Field (who against Worcestershire in 1914 took six wickets for two runs), W. C. Hands, S. P. Kinnear, A. A. Lilley, J. H. Parsons (a Gentleman and a Player), W. G. Quaife, S. Santall, E. J. Smith, F. G. Stephens, as well as F. R. Foster.

Little W. G. Quaife left Sussex for Warwickshire because he found it hard to get a job during the winter. He was an elegant pocket Hercules who played for Warwickshire in 1893 (making his first century at Edgbaston) and in 1928, in his only appearance in first-class cricket at the age of 56, bowed himself out with another century in his farewell game. He had played for Warwickshire for 35 years, and made 36,050 runs with 72 centuries to his credit, and an average of over 35. Only Grace, Woolley, Mead and Hobbs made their thousand runs a season more often than little W. G. Quaife. He was a mercurial field. He was with MacLaren's team in Australia; he also played in two Tests in England in 1899.

Then there were 'Tiger' Smith and the great Lilley. 'Dick' Lilley had a Test career stretching over 14 years. He played 31 times against Australia, and in those matches he caught 65 and stumped 19 of the foe. He played for Warwickshire for 23 years: beginning before the county was first-class. He caught 679 batsmen and stumped 204.

E. J. Smith was a junior partner to Barnes and Foster in Australia in 1911/12. He took over in Tests as substitute for Strudwick suffering from a ricked back, and 'Struddy' never could re-capture his place. Smith held a brilliant catch to get rid of Armstrong while Barnes was taking five for six at Melbourne and he marvellously stumped Hill on the leg-side to assist Foster in his 5–19. He was a fascinating batsman at times, especially against Hordern. He did not believe in letting a googly become a googly. He once charged half the length of the pitch to slam the bowler to the boundary – Hordern asked: 'Why don't you come and take the thing out of my hand?'

Well, such were some of the heroes of 1911. As Mr Ted Hampton, the Club's Honorary Statistician, has pointed out, Warwickshire was sixth in 1895, the year they entered the County Championship, fifth in 1901, and never higher until their victory in 1911: they reached a nadir in the previous three seasons, finishing 12th, 12th and 14th. In 1912 they were 9th and from 1919 to 1923 they were always in double figures from the top of the table. Indeed in the 23 seasons from 1919 to 1948 they were 16 times from 11th to 16th.

Then came better times. They were 7th in 1948, then 4th two years running – then first again! Tom Dollery was then in command, and among his great players were Martin Donnelly, though he was far away in the Championship year, F. C. Gardner, J. S. Ord, T. L. Pritchard, C. W. Grove and Eric Hollies: and I must mention J. R. Thompson who was, C. B. Fry told me, as handsome a bat as any he had seen since the Second World War. Nor must R. T. Spooner fail to get the highest accolade: good enough to get his thousand runs in a season and to keep wicket in seven Tests for England. What riches! What a side to lead to victory in 1951!

That team Tom Dollery captained won 16 county matches and lost only two: they beat Middlesex (twice) and Yorkshire by an innings. They called on only 14 men: not one of whom was picked for any of the five Tests against South Africa or for Gentlemen v. Players.

But Dollery was the solidest of county captains, and very many of his 1,491 runs were scored when there was the greatest need for them. Spooner, the left-hander, was confident, almost cheeky and made 1,767 for the county with an average of 43. His opening partner, Gardner, was firmly steady, and Ord was invaluable – doing much better than in the previous season. Hitchcock of New Zealand pulled and hooked admirably; and Wolton was often of importance in the middle batting.

The bowling was just good enough. Hollies took 145 county wickets for 17.69. Grove – an accurate seamer – was specially dangerous on a green 'un. Pritchard, after a disastrous start, and the 21-year-old slow left-hander Weeks, who took the place of the departed and excellent Abdul Hafeez Kardar, were of great value.

It was hard on Donnelly that he should have had no share in the season of triumph. He scored a double century for New Zealand in 1949 and was good enough to travel to Edgbaston just to watch his fielding at cover-point. But of course the mighty name in the side was that of Tom Dollery. He was an inspiring captain, cool, calm and shrewd. He was a grand, solid bat. He played in four Tests – far too few.

When you praise Dollery, you must not forget Hollies. He was the very best of *trundlers*. He had the figure for it – short, well-rounded but never tubby. He trotted to the wicket, whistled over his right arm and out shot a leg-break, good enough you will remember to take Bradman's wicket for nought in his last Test innings, when a score of four would have given him an average of 100. Hollies, who played in

13 Tests, was never as good elsewhere as he was on English wickets. He was 39 in the year of Tom Dollery's championship side, and five years before had taken 184 wickets, including all ten of Nottinghamshire without assistance from the field. From 1937 on he never failed to get 100 wickets in a season. There were some who professed to find him a poor field. He was surely as bad a bat as any in first-class cricket. In 1948 he knocked up 68 for Warwickshire with an average of 4.53. How difficult to choose between 1911 and 1951; for better or for worse, I go for 1911; how easily I might be wrong.

The third phase of Warwickshire's greatness came between 1959 (when they were fourth) and 1966. They were third in 1962, fourth in 1963, runners-up the next year, and sixth in 1964, Gillette Cup winners in 1966. Their chief batsman was M. J. K. Smith, the captain. He made his début for Leicestershire in 1951,captained Oxford in 1956, first played for Warwickshire in the same year, captained the side from 1957 to 1967, appeared in 47 Tests, captained England in 25, scored 1,000 runs in a season 14 times, and held 52 catches for Warwickshire in 1961 – a county record. In all (till the end of 1967) he made 31,580 runs with 55 centuries and an average of 41.99. He was a natural leader – a leader by example rather than exhortation, considering that men of proven ability did not need orders. He was never dull, and always played with his eye on the situation of the game. He had prodigious courage – a broken wrist was a handicap he soon overcame; and batting or fielding at short leg in spectacles was no trouble at all to one of only two Englishmen to have played both Rugby and cricket for England this century.

He had a *corps d'élite* at his command. R. W. Barber who joined the county from Leicestershire in 1962 was one of the very few leg-spinners to be picked for England since the war, and about the most fantastic hard-hitting batsman of our day. Those who saw it still speak with bated breath of his 185 in less than four hours in the third Test of 1965/6.

There were such splendid flying-buttresses of the middle-order as the New Zealand born Hitchcock, A. C. Smith the wicket-keeper, as well as wonderful openers in Horner and Ibadulla, and such run-getters as W. J. Stewart who first got his 2,000 in a season in 1962. And Cartwright, so great a medium-paced bowler that he was called to the first two Tests in 1968, though playing in neither (once because of injury). He is a very good batsman too. In 1962 he was the first Warwickshire man since F. R. Foster in 1914 to achieve the 'double'.

Then there was the marvellous victory in the Gillette Cup of 1966. They beat Worcestershire in the final. R. W. Barber was man of the match with his 66 and D. L. Amiss, a recent England player, made 44. Best of the bowlers was Cartwright with three good wickets for 16.

Yes, Warwickshire's batting potential has been and is phenomenal. So has been the fast-medium attack with Cartwright as its leader, but the spinners have been very thin on the ground till Lance Gibbs came to join the side in 1968. So far, he has not become the destroying force he can be.

Gibbs – and Kanhai! The two of them may well change the future of Warwickshire cricket and the very image of the county side in the public mind. Against Derbyshire last season Kanhai proved that he is a man who can shoulder responsibility and play for his side when others fail, as well as be the supreme artist at the batting crease. As to what Gibbs can do to help a side almost bankrupt in spin-bowling – well, imagination boggles at the prospect.

Yes, one can predict with confidence that Warwickshire in the early 'seventies may know its greatest era yet. It deserves it, for it is a county of traditions and not afraid of hard work – Deriek Taylor is doing much to educate young local cricketers in the Colts and Under-13 teams.

And the spirit of Warwickshire is loyal and hopeful. Mr L. T. Deakins, the general secretary, tells how in 1957, with Edgbaston back on the Test rota after 28 years, he rigged up a canvas chair in the centre pavilion for an 80-year-old member to get the very view he loved best. Next morning arrived a cheque for £500 and a courteous note saying this was payment on account for marvellous days in the sun long enjoyed at Edgbaston.

Warwickshire has had flashes of greatness in the past; but its future will be brighter still.

Chapter Sixteen

WORCESTERSHIRE, 1964

BY DENZIL BATCHELOR

The county all but achieved fame in its very first Championship match: for two-thirds of that game in May 1899 it out-played Yorkshire, leading by 211 to 139 on the first innings. The great figure was the sturdy, moustachioed Worcestershire opening bowler Wilson, who bowled round-arm and took eight for 70 in the first innings. But perhaps the greatest figure of all was the first county secretary, P. H. Foley, discovered feverishly painting the sight screens when the first over was bowled. Cricket was a more primitive state of life in those days: someone once counted 210 sheep, seven horses and three cows on the ground just before a match began.

Of course, in those days the county was known as Fostershire: except for two seasons – 1911–12, when G. H. Simpson-Hayward took over – one Foster or another captained the side from 1899 to 1913; and M. K. was to lead it from 1923 to 1925.

H. K. was a dashing batsman – all racquet strokes and rash drives. It was typical of him that in the Coronation Day match in August 1902 he should hit 125 in 85 minutes. He made over 13,000 runs for the county with an average of 35, while R. E. Foster hit over 5,000, averaging 47.68. W. L., M. K. and G. N. – later to play for Kent – were also great men in their day.

Incomparably the greatest Foster was R. E. – 'Tip' Foster as he was called in those days of nicknames. His 287 in his first Test match of all, at Sydney in the 1903/4 tour, was described by P. F. Warner, his captain, as incomparable for both off-hitting and driving. He took seven hours ten minutes to score his runs, hitting 80 in the last hour, and 37 fours in all. He was the most elegant of batsmen in the Golden Age, all lithe grace and steel springs, an artist in cover-drives and late-cuts. He scored a century for Oxford in the Varsity match followed by two for the Gentlemen at Lord's in 1900.

There were other Fosters. B. S., the actor, could give little time to the game, and N. J. A. played little as he worked abroad. Of course, there were others beside the Fosters. There was Fred Bowley, the stylist, who averaged over 30 when scoring 19,788 for the county. There were the aforementioned Wilson (725 wickets at 24 runs a-piece) in first-class cricket, and E. G. Arnold (1,079 wickets for 23 apiece) – a fine batsman too and another member of Warner's unexpectedly triumphant 1903/4 side in Australia.

They say H. K. Foster once heard Wilson grumbling about a pitch and said: 'Yes, of course it's no good to any bowler, but you'll go on and do your best till I take you off.' It would have led to a strike today but in those days was the prelude to a spell of 20 overs. That was the spirit of the side.

But I confess that before the coming of Root, Howarth, Flavell, Jenkins, Perks and Jackson, my favourite Worcestershire bowler was G. H. Simpson-Hayward, the renowned 'lobster'. He took 325 wickets for the county for 22 runs apiece. Unlike other lob-bowlers he bowled almost without trajectory and with a sharp off-break instead of spinning from the leg-side. He picked up the art through playing with billiard balls, went to South Africa in 1909/10, finished second to Blythe in the averages with 23 wickets for 18.26 apiece. He liked the matting wickets, and licked his lips at the sight of G. A. Faulkner, A. D. Nourse and G. C. White as opponents. Foster himself was not above teasing a boring batsman with lobs which went 30 feet up and were meant to drop on to the bails: a critic wrote to the secretary to ask if the batsmen might pursue such deliveries which generally dropped dead, and then play his shot – if necessary after they had dropped motionless behind the stumps?

Worcestershire's first Golden Age drew to its end; you could say this happened in 1908. The side finished near the top of the table in 1907 (as it did in 1962), but it had to wait for the captaincy of Don Kenyon and the summers of 1964 and '65 to win the title. But in the earliest days – even before the Golden Age was over – statistical triumph mattered little. It was when playing Worcestershire in 1904 that Sammy Woods was asked at Taunton how Somerset were doing in the County Championship Table. His reply ought to (but doesn't) serve as a model to all modern captains: 'Championship Table! I've never heard of it.'

The First World War took its toll of Worcestershire cricket. W. B. Burns was killed; and Frank Chester lost an arm, to become the most famous umpire of his day. The county took no part in the 1919 season, and by only two votes did the First Class counties allow the side to re-enter the field in 1920: so near to extinction did the Club come.

But under Maurice Foster, Fred Root achieved greatness in 1923. Root was the most willing warhorse that ever played county cricket. He shambled up to the wicket and bowled a late in-swinger which straightened up from the pitch. He took seven for 42 for the North of England against the 1926 Australians, and in the Lord's Test bowled H. L. Collins for a duck, and then had Macartney dropped at second slip before he had scored.

Gilbert Ashton, H. L. Higgins, J. B. Higgins and H. O. Rogers were all minor heroes before the '30s: and H. H. ('Doc') Gibbons and P. F. Jackson arrived on the scene they were to adorn for so long. Tarbox and Dick Pearson (who always vowed that the half-volley which 'did' a bit either way was the best of all balls) were two bowlers of great ability, and Major M. F. S. Jewell was a sterling captain in a period which was generally one of unmitigated disaster. The greatest of all Worcestershire statistical experts once wrote that 'as a bowler Jewell was disgraceful' but was forced to admit that he once took four wickets in five balls against Gloucestershire. He was a fair bat and a more than fair field, and a pillar of strength in his work for the county Club.

By the start of the '30s Worcestershire had a quiverful of imposing players. C. F. Walters joined the side as secretary-player in 1928: perhaps the most dashing batsman not named Foster ever to play for the county. He came from Glamorgan where he had won his spurs in youth, but it was when he came to Worcestershire, so often to partner 'Doc' Gibbons in breathtaking partnerships, that he was seen at his best. His retirement due to ill-health was one of the crippling blows the county suffered in the 1930s, together with the death from an enlarged heart of Nichol in his bed during the week-end of the Whitsun match with Essex in '34 at the age of 28.

On the happier side came the batting triumphs of Gibbons, below average height, and a massive cover-driver and cutter especially of slow bowlers, as well as a cover-point of genius. Jackson, once a medium-paced swinger and later an off-spinner of notable achievement, was an integral part of the Fred Root leg-trap. Nor must Bernard Quaife, son of Warwickshire's W. G., be forgotten – a wicket-keeper batsman of renown. Charles Bull, like Nichol, victim of an early death, had come from Kent to delight all who love quite fabulously acrobatic fielding.

The pride and joy of the side's attack, Fred Root, lost his form in '32, but in the following year the batting was vastly improved, and in '35 Perks, Howarth and Jackson came into their own, S. H. Martin batted admirably, and the side won nine matches. The county had entered the '30s next thing to penniless, but by the middle of the decade had won themselves such a reputation that they were a credit to the Championship competition.

Under Lord Cobham's captaincy (followed by that of A.

Captains all. *Above:* Brian Sellers (Yorkshire) (*left*) and A. W. Carr of Notts.
Below: Surrey's Stuart Surridge (*left*) and A. W. Richardson (Derbyshire)

Captains all. *Above:* Wilf Wooller, Glamorgan (*left*), and Walter Robins, Middlesex. *Below:* Worcestershire's Don Kenyon (*left*) and A. C. Ingleby-Mackenzie (Hampshire), whose inspiring enthusiasm is clearly evident here

P. Singleton) and in post-war years generally, Worcestershire entered into an era of greatness. Both in '46 and '47 they began the season by beating touring sides: India and South Africa respectively. Dick Howarth (picked for the Oval Test) was more than a great spin bowler – in '47 he took 164 wickets and made 1,150 runs. The coming of Don Kenyon was another major asset – he headed the 2,000 mark as early as 1950; the year after the county had finished fourth in the Championship, its highest place since 1899.

Among the glories of those days was the batting of the Nawab of Pataudi (senior), who heads the county's batting averages through the ages, scoring 2,381 runs in 44 completed innings: the only player to average over 50. Pataudi hit the best century I ever saw in a University match and the dullest I ever saw in a Test – his first innings against Australia with Jardine's team. His illness and return to India before the War were formidable handicaps for the team to overcome.

And, of course, this rich period was adorned by Roly Jenkins, Worcestershire incarnate, who lived every moment of his life for cricket. The author once travelled from Paddington to Totnes with him and he only broke off his monologue about the game once, when he looked out of the window and said 'Exeter'. He was a rustic bat and a leg-break bowler of renown as well as a dazzling fieldsman close to the wicket. He once did two hat-tricks in a match against Surrey; and in his long career took over 1,000 wickets for the county.

But let us linger over 1950 for a while. In that season, in his 43rd year, Howarth retired from county cricket, leading the bowling averages as he bowed himself out.

In '54 Kenyon scored his 2,000 for the fourth season running and his 22-year-old partner, Peter Richardson hit up 2,294 in his second full season. The following year the county, led for the only time by Perks, began the summer by beating the South African tourists largely due to the bowling of Martin Horton, who did the double for the first time that year.

Horton is Worcester born and bred, and played twice for England against India in 1959.

And so to 1964, *annus mirabilis*. I take it as the greatest Worcestershire side ever: a team of giants who won the Championship by a wide margin. Tom Graveney headed the batting averages, all elegance and splendour: two mailed fists within two velvet gloves. He became the first post-war batsman to hit 100 centuries: 13 of them for Worcester. Young Headley, a vastly improved batsman that season with a punishing drive: the first man in England to reach his 1,000 runs.

Third on the list of successful batsmen was the most important of all – Don Kenyon, the captain. He produced two centuries and three half-centuries in his last five matches; three of these innings were really vital to his side. He never looked at his best when batting for England: he was always too nervous, perhaps too modest. But he was a splendid driver, inspired and inspiring as a county captain.

Then there was D. W. Richardson, who began the season badly, but against Leicestershire, Nottingham and Essex – three important victories gained in August – did almost as well as Graveney himself. Horton also played admirably, hitting three centuries against the Universities and more half-centuries (11) than anyone except Graveney.

But looking back at that golden season, it was, I think, the bowlers who did it. Worcestershire has a long tradition of thankfulness to its attack from the round-armed G. Wilson and the 'lobster' G. H. Simpson-Hayward, and in 1937 the county had four in the side who took over 100 wickets each: R. Perks (141), S. H. Martin (114), R. Howarth (105) and P. F. Jackson (102). Again in '61, four more achieved the feat: J. A. Flavell (171), L. J. Coldwell (140), N. Gifford (133) and M. J. Horton (101); Flavell, Coldwell and Gifford at less than 20 runs apiece.

Coldwell, Flavell (this time 101 for 15.09) and Gifford were in the Champion side of 1964: indeed, they were the triple spearhead of the attack with 276 wickets between them in the Championship games, and all three with averages ranging from 14 to 17 runs apiece. Flavell and Coldwell were the best county openers in the game.

Coldwell began with seven for 53 against the Australians in their first innings, and in the first four matches actually took 27 wickets for 313. Flavell's greatest triumphs came in the last five county matches when he took 46 wickets for 539. All three were picked for England against Australia, each for two matches. Gifford spun the ball a good deal: some said he would have been an even greater slow left-hander if he had stood up straighter at the moment of delivery like Charlie Parker, J. C. White and Hedley Verity. All the same, he did as well as any English bowler in the Tests. He was also at his very best in the match against Leicestershire when, after three defeats in four games – the county's only losses – his bowling and Flavell's, with the batting of Graveney and Fearnley, did most to win the game. Standen's bowling – 52 wickets for 14.42 – was also wonderful; he became the third Worcestershire bowler to top the first-class averages. He embarked on the season having kept goal for West Ham United, winners of the F. A. Cup Final.

Perhaps 1965 was an even greater year, but I think not. Worcestershire won only one match in May; only one in June; and by July 23rd had only three victories to their credit. They then won ten out of their last 11 matches, beating Sussex in the final game to take the Championship by four points, Graveney averaging 68, d'Oliviera 43 and Headley, with over 1,300 runs for an average of 31, were the most successful batsmen. Flavell (132 wickets) was head and shoulders the best bowler: Coldwell (78 wickets) and Gifford (62) came a respectful distance behind.

In 1966 when Worcestershire were second in the County Championship – Graveney, d'Oliviera, Horton, Kenyon and Ormrod were their bright, particular stars – they lost the Gillette Cup in the final to Warwickshire after a splendid match. They were fifth in the County Table in '67.

I have picked the '64 team for my greatest Worcestershire XI in spite of the absence of d'Oliviera, because I believe its attack was the finest ever.

Here then, since a cricket team contains 11 men and no more, is my chosen Worcestershire side in batting order: D. Kenyon, M. J. Horton, R. G. A. Headley, T. W. Graveney, D. W. Richardson, J. A. Ormrod, R. Booth, J. A. Standen, N. Gifford, L. J. Coldwell and J. A. Flavell. I should be happy to see such a side represent not Worcestershire today – but England.

Chapter Seventeen

YORKSHIRE

BY DENZIL BATCHELOR

To think of anybody but A. A. Thomson writing in this book about Yorkshire calls for a degree of heretical imagination beyond the scope of the late Lord Habe. 'Tommie' contrived to be (with a sweet gentleness that we like to think typically southern) Scottish and Yorkshire in the same breath. I can but salute him, forget to be Scottish (which indeed I am, as much as English), and do my best for the county he loved above all others.

Yorkshire! It is a name synonymous with cricket itself. It seems incredible that from 1870 Yorkshire (formed in 1863) had to wait till 1893 before it again won the Championship. Victories in 1896 and 1898 were followed by a hat-trick in 1900/02, then came triumphs in 1905, '08, '12, '19, 1922/25, 1931/3, 1935, 1937/46 (the war years '40/'45 being omitted); thence into modern history with a tie shared with Middlesex in '49, and victories in '59, '60, '62, '63, '66, '67 and 1968. It is a record in outright County Championship wins; but I was never very good at the Higher Mathematics.

Their sides were so frequently immortal. In 1896, 'Jacker', Ted Wainwright, Lord Hawke and Bobby Peel scored four centuries in one innings against Warwickshire; among their very great early batsmen – before the 'fifties – who scored over 10,000 runs in their career were J. T. Brown, W. Barber, D. Denton, C. Hall. S. Haigh, Lord Hawke, Hirst, Holmes,

F. S. Jackson, Roy Kilner, Leyland, Mitchell, Oldroyd, Peel, Rhodes, Sutcliffe (headed by Hutton, with only Holmes and Leyland of the others bettering an average of 40), and Tunnicliffe. There were others.

Among the great early bowlers (over 500 wickets up to '49) were Bates, Bowes, Emmett, Ulyett, Haigh, Hirst, F. S. Jackson, Kilner, Macaulay, Peate, Peel, Rhodes, E. Robinson, Smailes, Verity, Wainwright (who appears in batsmen's and bowlers' lists) and Waddington.

Those were some of the 'ancients'. Among the moderns you will include Sir Leonard, Norman Yardley, Watson, Wardle, Boycott (the best living English batsman), Close, Illingworth – today's greatest English all-rounder – Freddie Trueman, the greatest character in post-war cricket, Binks (the most neglected post-war wicket-keeper). Among others yet to be saluted come R. A. Hutton, Padgett, Taylor and Hampshire: A. A. Thomson's particular young hero.

'Let us now praise famous men'. Well, we have done so, but we have left out many great names – George Freeman and Tom Emmett of old; later T. Taylor and Ernest Smith. They spring immediately to mind – and where has it got us? Nowhere. Precisely nowhere.

There are bookfuls to be written about the county, to begin with. No county team has done better – or even nearly as well against Yorkshire as Yorkshire has done against it. Yorkshire's all-rounders have been incomparable down the years.

Hirst has the greatest of all records to his credit – in 1906 he made 2,385 runs (average 45.86) and took 208 wickets (average 16.50). He did the double 14 times: Rhodes did it 16 times. Nobody else since the history of cricket began approaches those figures. It must be said that for thirty years one or other of them was not far off the greatest all-rounder in the game.

I remember being amused at the last Test in Yorkshire before the War against Australia when I found the crowds at Leeds in '38 streaming out of the ground uninterested by the Australians' victory to read the news of the *real* game: Surrey were on top of the county at the Oval. What were Verity and Bowes doing wasting their time in this pick-up game when they could have been bowling out Gregory and Fishlock and Whitfield?

I was wrong to be amused, and the Yorkshire crowd were right to be upset. *Theirs* was the real cricket. It was England's duty either to stage their Test Matches as Yorkshire v Australia or not to be surprised if nobody took any particular notice of what happened in these minor fixtures.

Look at the 1938 Yorkshire team which won the title for the eleventh time since the First War (the 22nd time in all). Sutcliffe and Hutton, Barber, Mitchell, Leyland, Sellers (captain – can you think of a better one?), Smailes, E. P. Robinson, Wood, Verity and Bowes. That's a Yorkshire team: and I have left out Norman Yardley.

Here's the English side that year at its best: Hutton, Barnett, Edrich, Hammond, Paynter, Compton, Ames, Verity, Sinfield, Wright and Farnes. Which would you back? I am not sure either.

Go right back to, say, 1912: when Yorkshire also won the Championship. England at the Oval against Australia were represented by: Hobbs, Rhodes, Spooner, Fry, Woolley, Hearne, Douglas, F. R. Foster, Smith, Barnes and Dean. A great side, indeed – but any better than say, R. R. Wilson (above Hirst and Kilner in the averages), Rhodes, Denton (average 53), Alonzo Drake, Hirst, Kilner, Haigh, Oldroyd, Booth, Sir A. White, Dolphin; I will give you Sir A. White who, *Wisden* said, was 'a very capable captain, always having his team well in hand.'

Yes, Yorkshire has been cricket history incarnate since they first took the field against Norfolk (with Fuller Pilch who first played the game in Sheffield) in 1833. They played county matches that didn't count in any League, but in the 'sixties George Freeman (whom W. G. named as the best fast bowler he ever saw) and the ever-laughing left-hander Tom Emmett made the side the first mighty name in cricket history. Tom invented the first unplayable ball, long before the googly or the chinaman. It pitched on the legs and hit the off stump and Tom called it the *sosteneuter*. Why, not even W. G. could pick it, though he was one man who could play Emmett, who admiringly said of him: 'I put the ball where I want it – and he puts it where he wants it.'

Yorkshire were far from the best team in England in the 'eighties: it was left to Ulyett – a great bowler who developed into a superb batsman, and to Lord Hawke to bring the county back to the top of the tree.

Lord Hawke and 'Jacker' were the only regular amateurs before the turn of the century when Frank Mitchell, E. R. Wilson and T. L. Taylor (all Cambridge players) joined them. Seven Yorkshiremen of the period played for England, but this by no means impresses *aficionados,* who all say that David Hunter was a better wicket-keeper than Lilley. As for Lord Hawke, I remember Charles Fry telling me that he was no better than anyone else as captain, but was a superb batsman.

If the 'nineties were good the turn of the century was better. The county were champions in '05 and in '08 and never in the first decade were lower than third. I think the 1908 side (which never lost one of its 33 matches) was one of the best the counties ever fielded, but it was surely no better than the earlier champions of '05.

People – envious people – sometimes say that Yorkshire comes first, England second. But it certainly wasn't so in 1905. F. S. Jackson was captain, won all five tosses, won the rubber, and headed the batting and bowling averages. He made 82 not out in the first Test, and took 5 for 52 in the first innings; he made 144 not out in the Leeds match; and 113 at Manchester. He averaged over seventy with the bat, just over fifteen as a bowler. Hirst, Rhodes, Haigh and Denton all played for England this year.

Over and over again a county team which was a mere

shadow of its full strength took the field: and in the very last match of '05 they were up against real trouble against Essex. J. W. H. T. Douglas got them out for 96, and on the last day they had a hideous task in the second innings to save the day. Hirst made 90 in five hours, and Ernest Smith (I met him as a preparatory schoolmaster at Eastbourne) came in at number eight with an hour to go. He was about the biggest hitter of the day, but this was no time for the long handle. He batted for an hour, was undefeated, did not break his duck – and did as much as anyone to make sure of the Championship.

Hirst was not yet the leading all-rounder in the country, 'but', says A. A. Thomson, 'his stride was lengthening.'

No county match in any season can compare with the Roses Match, and the 1905 game was one of the greatest ever. Hirst took 5 for 66 and 4 for 49, and when Yorkshire's batting faltered, he rallied the ranks with an aggressive 74, which had as much as anything to do with Yorkshire's 44-run victory.

Ah, that Roses Match! Yorkshire's four years of dominance from 1922/25 held an example of such a battle which remains fadeless in memory. It was, as Tommie has said, one of the first of the safety-first matches when the object was not to score runs but 'to prevent the other side from scoring any.' Roy Kilner summed up these battles of attrition. What was wanted he said 'is no umpires and fair cheating all round.'

Well, this return Roses match of 1922 was the supreme example of the new sort of cricket. Yorkshire were set 132 on the last day. Wickets fell with terrible regularity. When Rhodes came in at Number 5 he had to defend for his life – he knew that his skipper Geoffrey Wilson was absent ill. When Rockley Wilson came in, last man to bat, six runs were needed. The light was worsening: not so the bowling. Three runs were made in 5 overs.

Rhodes played the last over with three needed to win. He played the first five balls carefully – no run there. Down came the last ball of the match. It turned to the off – and Rhodes left it alone.

That will give you a little picture of the philosophy of the Roses Match and of the men who play in it – who ever heard of a Test being taken quite as seriously?

It is impossible in this space to do justice to Hirst and Rhodes, surely the two greatest players who ever gave their lives, hearts and souls to Yorkshire, or to any county. Hirst played for Yorkshire from 1891 to 1921. He scored 36,203 runs with an average of 34.05 and took 2,739 wickets for 18.72 runs.

Rhodes first appeared in 1898 and last played in 1930. His 39,797 runs gave him an average of 30.70. His 4,187 wickets were taken at 16.71 apiece.

After they left the scene Yorkshire won eight championships out of ten from 1931 to 1946 – the War years excluded. In the 'fifties came the period dominated by Surrey and Surridge, and finally from '59 on there have been seven Yorkshire victories in ten years.

In the 'thirties the immortals were Sellers, the most forceful captain of his (or perhaps any) day; the incomparable Sutcliffe, Verity – most thoughtful and glorious of all left-hand bowlers. Bowes, a great fast and a great seam bowler, Mitchell, the immemorial E. P. Robinson, Leyland, Macaulay, Wood, Hutton (a chapter in England's book of glory), Yardley and Holmes.

I defy anyone to choose unarguably the greatest Yorkshire side of this era: there will be more agreement – though not unanimous at that – as to whether when you have chosen it, you have picked about the best side that ever played Championship cricket.

I will pick the side that in the year of the Second World War won the Roses Match at Old Trafford by an innings and 43 runs. Here is the batting order with one change: Sutcliffe, Hutton, Mitchell, N. W. Yardley, Barber, Leyland, A. B. Sellers, Wood, Robinson, Verity, Bowes. (I have brought in Leyland, who was not available, for Turner).

Yorkshire – by Denzil Batchelor

And so to the latest – assuredly not the last – chapter of Yorkshire's greatness – the post-Surrey years from '59 on when Yorkshire have fielded under D. B. Close a side that has rarely been less good than the Rest of England. Close is an astute, aggressive captain: Yorkshire to the marrow of his bones. Boycott is the solidest, noblest, best of post-war English batsmen: a worthy successor to Sutcliffe and Sir Leonard – you can't say fairer than that. Sharpe, not least for his fielding, has become the unluckiest of English batsmen. Illingworth is the solidest all-rounder you could ask for – the Yorkshire side without him will be unrecognisable. Binks is one of the best of wicket-keepers: I have seen him take leg-side falling catches last summer that I would hardly have believed of Godfrey Evans.

As for Fred Trueman – words fail me though I might be able to do justice to Lindwall or Larwood. Fred told me once, the first time I met him, that as a boy he had tramped from Leeds to Nottingham just to cast his eyes on Larwood – and him with one leg shorter than the other. I think it can be said of him that while he was in the side you could never wipe off English cricket as a spent force.

As for Padgett, Hampshire, Taylor – they would be beyond praise in other county sides. And Wilson is as magnificent a bowler as ever got the dazzling fielding he deserves.

Oh yes – they are incomparable! If there were further Triangular Tests and I was the South African captain, I should be as pleased about beating Yorkshire as I should be about overcoming Australia, let alone England.

Why have they only once won the Gillette Cup? Probably because they consider it some Southern fall-lall, something as unimportant as the Derby compared with the St Leger, which cannot be spoken of in the same breath as the all-important County Championship.

I'm sorry for all the superlatives, Tommie my dear. But we did agree, didn't we, that there's only one Yorkshire?

INDEX

Abel, R., 90
Alderman, A. E., 13, 17
Allen, G. O., 15, 80
Allen, M. H. J., 70
Alley, W. E., 85–6
Ames, L. E. G., 41, 79, 119
Amiss, D. L., 107
Andrew, K. V., 68–70
Armstrong, W. W., 48, 103–4
Arnold, E. G., 110
Arnold, P., 69
Ashton, G., 111
Astill, E., 53–5
Atkinson, C. R. M., 85, 87–8
Atkinson, G. G., 85–6
Austin, H. B. G., 71
Avery, A. V., 18

Bailey, T. E., 18, 76
Baker, C. S., 103
Baldrey, D. O., 32–3
Barber, R. W., 106–7
Barber, W., 117–18, 122
Barlow, R. G., 47
Barnard, H. M., 31–3
Barnes, S. F., 98, 102–4, 119
Barnes, W., 76
Barnett, C. J., 15, 36–7, 119
Barratt, F., 76–7, 79–80
Barrick, D. W., 69
Barrington, K. F., 92, 94
Bates, W., 118
Bedser, A. V., 73, 92–4, 98
Bedser, E. A., 73, 92–3
Berry, L., 55
Bestwick, W., 16
Binks, J. G., 123
Birkenshaw, J., 56–7
Blythe, C., 42, 44, 46, 52, 110
Bonnor, G. J., 39
Booth, B. J., 56–7
Booth, R., 116, 118
Bowes, W. E., 101, 118–19, 122
Bowley, E. H., 98–101
Bowley, F., 110
Boycott, G., 69, 123
Bradman, D. G., 21, 26, 37, 50, 55, 62, 66, 75, 105
Braund, L. C., 82–4
Brearley, W., 23, 48
Briggs, J., 47
Brockwell, W., 90
Broderick, 72
Brookes, V. D., 68–9
Brown, F. R., 68
Brown, J. T., 117
Brown, S. M., 62–3, 65

Bull, C., 112
Bull, F. G., 19, 22–3
Burden, M. D., 32
Burgess, A., 85, 87
Burns, W. B., 111
Burnup, C. J., 43
Bush, J. A., 38, 40
Bush, R. E., 38, 40
Buswell, W. A., 71

Carpenter, H., 19–20
Carr, A. W., 76–8
Carr, D. W., 43–4
Cartwright, T., 34, 107
Chapman, A. P. F., 34, 41, 78, 80, 84
Charlesworth, C., 103
Chester, F., 111
Clark, T. H., 92
Clay, J. C., 24–5, 27–9
Clayton, G., 85, 88
Clift, P., 25–6, 28
Close, D. B., 14, 38, 123
Cobham, Lord, 112
Coe, S., 54–5
Coldwell, L. J., 114–16
Collins, H. C., 111
Compton, D. C. S., 20, 25, 60–4, 66, 86, 119
Compton, L. H., 62, 64
Constable, B., 92–3
Constantine, L., 22, 65
Cook, T. E., 98, 100–1
Copson, W. H., 13–17
Cornford, J., 101
Cornford, W., 98–100
Cotter, A., 79
Cotton, J., 56, 58
Cowdrey, M. C., 41, 91
Cox, G., 95, 101
Crawford, J. N., 54
Crawford, V. F. S., 54
Crump, B., 69
Cuttell, W. R., 47–8

Dacre, C. C., 36–7
Davies, E., 25–6
Davies, H. G., 25, 27
Day, A. P., 43
Deakins, L. T., 107
Dean, H., 119
Denton, D., 117, 119–20
Denton, J. S., 71, 73
Denton, W. H., 71, 73
Derbyshire, 13–17, 31, 78, 107
Dexter, E. R., 45, 95
Dillon, E. W., 42, 44
Dipper, A. E., 36–7
d'Oliviera, B., 115–16

Dollery, H. E., 69, 102, 104-6
Dolphin, A., 119
Donnelly, M., 104-5
Douglas, J. W. H. T., 119, 121
Drake, A., 119
Duckworth, G., 48, 51, 79
Dudleston, B., 56-7
Duleepsinhji, K. S., 41, 96-8, 100-1
Durston, F. J., 61-2

Eagar, D., 21
Eaglestone, J., 25-6
Earle, G. F., 84
East, W., 71-3
Eckersley, P. T., 48, 51-2
Edrich, W. J., 20, 25, 60-4, 66, 86, 119
Elliott, C. S., 13, 17
Elliott, H., 13, 15, 17
Emmett, T., 118, 120
Essex, 18-23, 26, 114, 121
Evans, T. G., 58, 123

Fairservice, W. J., 42, 44, 46
Fane, F. L., 19-20
Farnes, K., 119
Farrimond, W., 51
Faulkner, G. A., 110
Fearnley, C., 115
Fender, P. G. H., 16, 90
Field, F. E., 103
Fielder, A., 42, 44, 46
Filgate, C. R., 38, 40
Firth, J., 55
Fishlock, L., 119
Flavell, J. A., 114-16
Fletcher, D., 92
Flowers, W., 76
Foley, P. H., 109
Foster, B. S., 110
Foster, F. R., 102-4, 107, 119
Foster, G. N., 109
Foster, H. K., 109-10
Foster, M. K., 109, 111
Foster, N. J. A., 110
Foster, R. E., 83, 109-10
Foster, W. L., 109
Freeman, G., 37, 42, 118-19
Fry, C. B., 14, 50, 72, 95-6, 104, 119-20

Gardner, F. C., 104-5
Geary, G., 53, 55
Gibbons, H. E., 111-12
Gibbs, L., 107
Gifford, N., 114-16
Gilbert, W. R., 38-9
Gilligan, A. E. R., 78, 96
Gimblett, H., 82-3
Gladwin, C., 16
Glamorgan, 24-9, 54, 68, 112
Gloucestershire, 14, 36-41, 43, 70, 75, 112

Goddard, T. W., 36-7
Goodwin, J., 55
Grace, E. M., 14, 28, 36, 38-9, 75
Grace, G. F., 38-40, 75
Grace, W. G., 14, 28, 36-40, 45, 47, 50, 58, 66, 75-6, 83, 103, 119-20
Graveney, T. W., 114-16
Gray, J. R., 31-3
Gray, L., 62, 64-5
Green, L., 48, 50-2
Gregory, J., 45, 49, 79-80, 119
Griffith, C., 45
Grimmett, C., 52
Grove, C. W., 104-5
Gunesekara, C. H., 62
Gunn, G., 75-8
Gunn, W., 76

Habe, Lord, 117
Haig, N., 61-2
Haigh, S., 46, 60, 117-20
Hall, C., 117
Hall, W., 45
Hallam, M. R., 53-6, 76
Hallows, C., 48-50
Hallows, J., 48
Hammond, W. R., 36-7, 41, 50, 62, 100, 119
Hampshire, 25, 28, 30-5, 57, 86
Hampshire, J., 118, 123
Hampton, E., 104
Hands, W. C., 103
Hardinge, H. T. W., 42-3
Harrison, L., 31, 33
Hawke, Lord, 54, 59, 84, 117, 120
Hayward, T., 20
Haywood, R. A., 71, 73
Headley, R. G. A., 114-16
Hearne, J. W., 60-2, 119
Heath, M., 32
Hendren, E. P., 50, 61-2, 65
Hever, N. G., 25, 27
Hewett, H. T., 86
Higgins, H. L., 111
Higgins, J. B., 111
Hill, A., 39
Hill, C., 103-4
Hill, N., 57
Hirst, G. H., 45-7, 53-4, 60, 83, 117-22
Hitch, B., 90, 102
Hitchcock, R. E., 105, 107
Hobbs, J. B., 49-50, 62, 64, 72, 75, 90-1, 99, 102-3, 119
Hollies, E., 104-6
Holmes, P., 117-18, 122
Hopwood, L., 52
Hornby, A. H., 47-8
Hornby, A. N., 38, 48
Horden, H. V., 103-4
Horner, N. F., 107

Horton, H., 31–3
Horton, M. J., 113–16
Howarth, R., 110, 112–14
Hubble, J., 44
Huish, F. H., 42–5
Humphreys, E., 42–3
Hunter, D., 120
Hutchings, K. L., 41–5
Hutton, L., 51, 64, 86, 118–19, 122–3

Ibadulla, W., 107
Iddon, J., 48–9
Ikin, J., 52
Illingworth, R., 123
Ingleby-Mackenzie, A. C. D., 31–2, 35
Inman, C. C., 56–7
Insole, D. J., 18

Jackson, F. S., 83, 117–18, 120
Jackson, J., 16, 22
Jackson, P. F., 110–12, 114
Jackson, V. E., 55
Jardine, D. R., 16, 50, 62
Jenkins, R., 86, 110, 113
Jessop, G. L., 37, 41
Jewell, M. F. S., 111–12
Johnson, P. R., 82–3
Jones, A. O., 45, 76, 78
Jones, J., 91
Jones, W. E., 25–7
Jupp, V., 68, 72

Kanhai, R., 33, 107
Kardar, A. H., 105
Kelleher, H. R. A., 70
Kelleway, C. E., 103
Kennedy, A., 31
Kent, 26, 41–6, 56, 71, 73, 87, 97, 109
Kenyon, D., 111, 113–16
Kermode, A., 48
Key, K. F., 90
Kilner, R., 16, 118–19, 121
King, J. H., 54–5
Kinnear, S. P., 103
Kitchen, M., 85–6
Knight, A., 54–5
Knott, A., 57, 64
Knott, F. H., 44
Kortright, C. J., 19, 22–3, 79

Laker, J. C., 90, 92–4
Lancashire, 18–19, 22, 36, 38, 47–52, 56,
    66, 68, 71, 73, 87–8, 99
Langford, B., 86–7
Langridge, James, 98–100
Langridge, John, 98, 100–1
Larter, J. D. F., 69
Larwood, H., 16, 46, 49, 65, 76–7, 79–80,
    123

Lee, H. W., 61–2
Leicestershire, 32, 53–9, 93, 106, 114–15
Lester, G., 55
Leyland, M., 118–19, 122
Lightfoot, A., 69
Lilley, A. A., 79, 103–4, 120
Lilley, B., 76, 78
Lindwall, R. R., 27, 49, 123
Livingston, L., 69
Livingstone, D. A., 31–3
Llewellyn, C. B., 30–1
Loader, P. J., 92, 94
Lock, G. A. R., 34, 56, 58–9, 90, 92–4
Lockwood, W., 21–3, 90
Lohmann, G., 90
Longman, H. K., 62
Lucas, A. P., 19
Lyon, B. H., 36–7
Lyon, M. D., 88

Macartney, C. G., 111
Macauley, G. G., 118, 122
MacBryan, J. C. W., 82–3
McCabe, S. J., 62
McDonald, E. A., 45–6, 48–9, 51, 79–80
McGahey, C. P., 19–22
MacGregor, G., 60
McIntyre, A. J., 92–4
MacLaren, A. C., 47–8, 103
Makepeace, H., 49–51
Mann, F. G., 62, 64
Mann, F. T., 60, 62
Manning, J. S., 70
Marner, P. T., 56–7
Marshall, R. E., 31–2, 34–5
Martin, S. H., 112, 114
Martyn, J., 82, 88
Mason, F. R., 42–4
Mason, J. R., 45
Matthews, T. G., 38–40
May, P. B. H., 45, 89–90, 92–3
Mead, P., 31, 33, 103
Mead, W., 19, 22–3
Melville, A., 101
Mercer, J., 24
Meyer, R. J. O., 87
Middlesex, 13, 26, 32, 60–7, 71, 105, 117
Midwinter, W. E., 38
Milburn, C., 69, 73, 76
Miles, R. F., 38, 40
Miller, K. R., 27
Minnett, R. B., 103
Mitchell, F., 118–20, 122
Mitchell, T. B., 13–16
Moberley, W. O., 38–9
Mold, A., 47
Muncer, L. B., 25–7
Munden, V. S., 55
Murrell, H. R., 62
Mynn, A., 47

Neale, W. L., 36
Newman, J., 31
Nichol, M., 112
Nichols, M. S., 18–19
Norman, M. E., 56, 69
Northamptonshire, 56, 68–74, 97
Nottinghamshire, 28, 35, 56, 58, 75–81, 114
Nourse, A. D., 110

Oates, T., 79
O'Connor, J., 18
Odell, W. W., 54
Oldroyd, E., 118–19
Ord, J. S., 104–5
Ormrod, J. A., 115–16
Owen, H. G., 19–20

Padgett, D. E. V., 118, 123
Palairet, L. C. M., 82–3, 86
Palmer, C. H., 55
Palmer, K. E., 85–7
Parker, C. W. L., 36–7, 115
Parkhouse, W. G. A., 25–6, 28
Parkin, C., 52
Parks, H., 99
Parks, H. W., 98, 100
Parks, J., 99
Parks, J. H., 98–100
Parsons, J. H., 103
Pataudi, N. of, 113
Paynter, E., 51, 119
Payton, W. G. E., 78
Payton, W. R. D., 75–8
Pearson, D., 111
Peate, E., 16, 118
Peel, R., 16, 59, 117–18
Perks, R., 110, 112–14
Perrin, P. A., 19–22
Pickett, H., 19
Pilch, F., 119
Pilling, H., 99
Pleass, J., 25–6
Poidevin, L. O. S., 48
Ponsford, W. H., 62
Poore, R. H., 30
Pope, A. V., 13–14, 16
Pope, G., 14, 16–17
Pougher, A. D., 53
Prideaux, R. M., 69
Pritchard, T. L., 104–5

Quaife, B., 112
Quaife, W. G., 102, 112

Ranjitsinhji, K. S., 41, 44, 46, 95–7
Rawlin, J., 60
Read, M., 90
Read, W., 90
Relf, A., 95

Reynolds, B. L., 68–9
Rhodes, H., 16
Rhodes, W., 37, 43, 45–6, 51–3, 60, 83–4, 103, 118–22
Richardson, A. W., 13–15
Richardson, D. W., 114, 116
Richardson, P., 113
Richardson, T., 21–3, 49, 79, 90
Riches, N. V. H., 24
Rippon, A. D. E., 73
Rippon, A. E. S., 73
Robertson, J. D., 62–4
Robertson-Glasgow, R. C., 85
Robins, R. W. V., 62, 64–6
Robinson, E. P., 17, 118–19, 122
Robinson, P. J., 85, 87
Rogers, H. O., 111
Root, F., 110–12
Rumsey, F., 86, 88
Rushby, T., 90
Russell, A. C., 22
Russell, T. M., 19, 22

Sainsbury, P. J., 31–3
Sandham, A., 16, 61, 77
Santall, S., 103
Scott, M. E., 69
Scott, R. S. G., 98, 100
Scotton, W. H., 76
Seabrook, F. J., 36–7
Sellers, A. B., 14, 24, 37, 89, 91, 94, 119, 122
Seymour, James, 42–4, 73
Seymour, John, 71, 73
Shackleton, D., 32, 34–5
Sharp, J., 48
Sharpe, P., 100, 123
Shaw, A., 78
Shepherd, T. F., 16
Sherwin, M., 76
Shrewsbury, A., 76
Shuter, J. K., 90
Sibbles, F. M., 48–9
Simpson-Hayward, G. H., 109–10, 114
Sims, J., 62, 64–7
Sinfield, R. A., 36–7, 119
Singleton, A. P., 113
Skeet, C. H. L., 62
Skelding, A., 21, 53
Smailes, T. F., 118–19
Smith, A. C., 107
Smith, C., 48
Smith, D., 13–15
Smith, E., 118–19, 121
Smith, E. J., 103–4
Smith, H., 36–7
Smith, M. J. K., 86, 106
Smith, P., 18
Smith, R., 18–19
Smith, S. G., 71–3

Index

Sobers, G., 33, 81
Somerset, 17, 32, 35, 68, 82–8, 111
Spencer, C. T., 55–6, 58
Spooner, R. H., 48, 83, 119
Spooner, R. T., 104–5
Standen, J. A., 115–16
Staples, A., 76–7, 79–80
Staples, S. J., 76–7, 79–80
Statham, J. B., 34, 52, 93
Steele, D. S., 69
Stephens, W. G., 103
Stephenson, H. W., 88
Stevens, G. T. S., 61–2
Stewart, M. J., 92, 94
Stewart, W. J., 107
Stoddart, A. E., 45
Storer, H., 13
Strudwick, H., 64, 99, 104
Sugg, F. H., 47
Sully, H., 69
Surrey, 14, 16, 18–21, 26, 28, 46, 48, 52, 56, 58, 64, 68, 75, 79, 85, 89–94, 113, 122–3
Surridge, W. S., 14, 24, 26, 89, 91–2, 94, 122
Sussex, 41, 55, 57, 61, 68, 95–101, 103, 115
Sutcliffe, H., 50, 62, 101, 118–19, 122–3

Tarbox, C. V., 111
Tate, F., 95
Tate, M. W., 90, 95–101
Tattersall, G., 52
Taylor, D., 107
Taylor, R., 31
Taylor, T. L., 118, 120, 122
Tennyson, L., 31, 34
Thompson, A., 62, 64
Thompson, G. J., 71–3
Thompson, J. R., 104
Thomson, I., 95–6
Timms, B., 33
Tolchard, R. W., 56–7
Tompkin, N., 55
Townsend, D. C. L., 39
Townsend, F., 38–9
Townsend, G. L., 39
Townsend, L. F., 13–16
Tray, D., 79
Tremlett, M. F., 82, 85
Tribe, G. E., 70, 72
Trick, S., 27
Trott, A., 60, 73
Trueman, F. S., 17, 22, 34, 55, 79, 93, 123
Trumper, V. T., 44–5, 95
Tunnicliffe, J., 83, 100, 118
Turnbull, M., 24
Turner, A. J., 19, 22
Turner, C., 122
Tyldesley, E., 48–50
Tyldesley, J. T., 47–50
Tyldesley, R., 48–51

Tyler, E. F., 82, 84
Tyson, F., 79
Tyson, F. H., 70

Ulyett, G., 118, 120

Verity, H., 16, 84, 101, 115, 118–19, 122
Vials, G. A. T., 71, 74
Virgin, R., 85–6
Voce, W., 76–7, 79–80

Waddington, A., 118
Wainwright, E., 59, 117–18
Walden, F., 71, 73
Walsh, F. E., 55
Walters, C. F., 24, 111
Ward, A., 47
Warner, P. F., 60–1, 72, 110
Warren, A. R., 16
Warwickshire, 11, 34, 61, 69, 102–8, 11., 115, 117
Washbrook, C., 52, 64
Wass, T., 76
Wassell, A., 32
Watkins, A. L., 25–8
Watson, F., 48–51
Watts, P. D., 69
Watts, P. J., 69
Weeks, R. T., 105
Wellard, A. W., 82–3
Wells, W., 71, 73
Wensley, A. F., 97–101
White, A., 119
White, D. W., 32
White, G. C., 110
White, J. C., 82, 84, 115
Whitfield, E. W., 119
Whysall, W. W., 76–8
Wilson, E. R., 119–21, 123
Wilson, G., 109–10, 114
Wilson, Geoffrey, 121
Wolton, A. V., 105
Wood, A., 84, 119, 122
Wood, C. J. B., 54–5
Woodfull, W. M., 62
Woods, S., 37, 82, 84, 111
Wooller, W., 24–8
Woolley, C. N., 71, 73
Woolley, F. E., 41–6, 50, 58, 71, 103, 11.
Worcestershire, 11, 33, 55, 68–9, 86–7., 103, 107, 109–16
Worthington, T. S., 13, 15
Wright, D. V. P., 119
Wynyard, E. G., 30

Yardley, N. W., 119, 122
Yorkshire, 11, 13–14, 16, 18–19, 30–1, 37., 39–41, 43, 46, 48, 54–5, 57, 60, 64., 68–70, 79, 84, 87, 90–1, 101, 105, 109., 117–23
Young, J. A., 62, 64–5